Living Stones

Living Stones

Involving Every Member in Ministry

Dr. Earl V. Comfort

STANDARD PUBLISHING

Cincinnati, Ohio   18-03179

Library of Congress Cataloging in Publication Data

Comfort, Earl V.
　Living stones: involving every member in ministry/by Earl V. Comfort.
　　p. cm.
　Bibliography: p.
　Includes index.
　ISBN 0-87403-249-0
　1. Pastoral theology. 2. Church growth. 3. Preaching. 4. Lay ministry. 5. Jacksonville Chapel (Lincoln Park, N.J.) I. Title.
BV4011.C63 1988
253 – dc19　　　　　　　　　　　　　　　　　　　　　　　88-12168
　　　　　　　　　　　　　　　　　　　　　　　　　　　　　　　　CIP

Copyright ©1988, The STANDARD PUBLISHING Company,
　Cincinnati, Ohio.
A division of STANDEX INTERNATIONAL Corporation.
Printed in U.S.A.

to my wife JoAnn,
my partner in the ministry

Foreword

A sleeping giant has been awakened in North Jersey. Jacksonville Chapel has grown more than six hundred percent under Dr. Earl Comfort's Biblical approach to the ministry.

My involvement at Jacksonville Chapel coincided with the coming of the Comforts to this ministry. The first Body Life meeting was initiated in our home. This was a forerunner to the zone ministry. It met the needs of the otherwise lonely individual in the midst of a large and growing congregation. What joy it has been to have witnessed the spiritual growth of many new believers who early began to share through the zone program.

Pastor Comfort's enthusiasm for Jesus Christ has been contagious and has fostered growth among the many facets of church ministry. The high percentage of its members involved in the ministry at Jacksonville Chapel is foundational to its success. This book explains how it all happened. Gifted Biblical teaching from the pulpit attracted spiritually hungry people. The "bandwagon" attraction of a living and moving work caused many people to participate in various facets of opportunity and outreach.

Organization along Biblical teaching is a major strength of the church. However, the person in the pew sees the fruit of that organization and not the detailed structure.

Pastor Comfort's dedication of himself to the service of pastor-teacher allowed the development of discipleship among many in the congregation. This approach equipped the saints for the work of ministry. The impact is being felt around the world.

Although there are many large churches in the world, few have such a large percentage of their people actually involved in ministry. It can happen in your congregation. Read this book with a prayer that the Holy Spirit will help you adapt these concepts to your church's needs.

Bill Tarter, President
International Missions, Inc.

Contents

Introduction

Upon graduation from Dallas seminary I had the firm conviction that if you preached the Word and remained free from sin and apostasy, your church would grow and prosper. But in my first church ministry I was thrown into a situation in which both the church and I expected far more than simply preaching and purity. I soon faced a heavy counseling schedule, did both hospital and evangelistic visitation, taught VBS, led teacher-training classes, attended endless board meetings, and even led singing.

As I look back I shake my head in wonder that I could have expended such energy, but I also hang my head in shame. I could certainly have accepted Snyder's indictment, "If the pastor is a superstar, then the church is an audience, not a body."[1] Ray Stedman could have been thinking of me when he wrote, concerning the "superstar" ministry, "This unbiblical distortion has placed pastors under an unbearable burden. They have proved completely unequal to the task of evangelizing the world, ministering to the poor and needy, relieving the oppressed and afflicted, expounding the Scriptures, and challenging the entrenched forces of evil in an increasingly darkened world. They were never meant to do it. To even attempt it is to end up frustrated, exhausted, and emotionally drained."[2]

As attendance increased, my work load also increased, to the point that I was even losing the joy of preaching the Word. I found myself suffering psychologically, physically, and spiritually. Dallas had trained me to preach, but I knew nothing about discipleship or the remarkable philosophy of Ephesians 4:11, 12. I had not the faintest concept of the distribution of ministry to the saints or my role as an equipper.

Then in the late 1960s and early 1970s some books began to jog my mind. I read Richards's *New Face for the Church* and some articles by Ray Stedman having to do with his *Body Life* concepts in California. I also made a major pastoral change at this time. I moved from a twelve-year ministry in South Jersey to a new ministry in North Jersey. It was not only a geographical but a cultural change. South Jersey was a rural retirement culture; North Jersey was as aggressive suburban area where things never slowed down.

The members of my new congregation were inventive, restless, and eager to grow. I felt a great stirring in my heart, because they expected me to preach the Word and not be engaged in too much else. Although the Jacksonville Chapel had a traditional background, I saw an eagerness for any change that would be Biblically valid.

During this time I continued a heavy reading schedule, especially of books having to do with church renewal. Many of them were froth, focused on an existential Christianity, but some had sound exegetical foundations that moved me deeply. I saw that even though I was suffering, it was actually I who had robbed the church. If what I was reading was true, I was violating Biblical principles and denying the people of God the ministry that actually belonged to them.

I had failed my previous church to some extent because I had been wrong in interpreting my role. Stedman again points the finger as he says, ". . . this distortion has resulted in a sadly impoverished church which has made little impact on the world and increasingly withdraws into impotent isolation. Nothing is more desperately needed than to return to the dynamic of the early church."[3]

I did not want to fail in my new pastorate. I was beginning to believe that this congregation was truly gifted in many areas in which I was not gifted. Snyder's words rebuked me as he talked about the mythical Pastor Jones, who had accepted the traditional role of a pastor. "Looking into the lives of several hundred members of Pastor Jones' church, one makes a startling discovery: every one of Pastor Jones' talents is equaled or surpassed by someone in the membership. A wealth of gifts lies buried because these talents are seemingly not needed."[4]

Surely there were people in the congregation who could perform all the various aspects of ministry that I was attempting to do better than I could. If I understood the Bible correctly, its message to me was this: Do not let all those talents lie buried and unused. When I usurped the ministry all to myself I was doing three things—ruining myself, robbing the congregation, and restricting the ministry of the body of Christ.

Wow! I had to change, and there had to be a means of organization that would reflect that change and facilitate the ministry.

---

[1]Taken from *The Problem of Wineskins* by Howard A. Snyder. ©1975 by InterVarsity Christian Fellowship of the USA and used by permission of InterVarsity Press, P.O. Box 1400, Downers Grove, IL 60515

[2]Ray Stedman, *Body Life*. Glendale, CA: Regal Books, 1972, p. 79. Used by permission.

[3]*Ibid.*

[4]Snyder, p. 82.

CHAPTER 1

The Problem

"God must have created the church," critics will say from time to time. "Otherwise, how could it possibly have survived over the centuries?" Beset with so many problems and such organizational chaos, the struggling church tests the allegiance of even its most loyal advocates.

Though we might agree with such a statement, we should not be too quick to condemn ourselves. Even the largest and most successful business institutions face similar difficulties. Corporate executives constantly reshuffle their organizations and make neverending but increasingly complex adjustments. It is not at all unusual for large corporations to be skating near the edge of disaster. "The reason so many small companies fail," stated a vice president of a major corporation, "is not a lack of business opportunities, but a lack of efficient organization."

Organization must be sharpened constantly, like a knife or an axe, because its fine edge is dulled through use and abuse. The church of Jesus Christ is not alone in its awareness of the need for shaping up.

The Nature of Church Work

Two common factors faced by every congregation have direct bearing on every major undertaking of the church. The first is considered to be an advantage, the second a liability.

Divine Mandate

The advantage is that since the church operates under a divine mandate, it does not have to try to discover or justify its reason for existence. The church can and should know what it is supposed to be and do.

A somewhat oversimplified statement of the task given the apostles and early church leaders can be described by the phrase, "Preach the Word!" This God-given purpose dare not be altered by man. The church, by knowing its mission in the world, can better fulfill its ministry more readily through deeper commitment to doing the will of the Lord.

Voluntary Labor

The disadvantage is that the church's labor force is largely voluntary, a situation seldom existing in the business world. Volunteerism presents its own set of problems.

The average work week of the leaders of my church, including commuting time, is sixty hours. That's half again more than the customary work period. What little time remaining has to be divided among family, recreation, chores, rest, and ministry. We could well be adding to an already troublesome burden if we encouraged the commitment of more time to the church.

Even in the best churches, ninety percent of the work is accomplished by less than one-third of the members. A core group of willing and dedicated volunteers accepts the greater share of the work of the church. Their volunteer ministries are not usually restful or relaxed times for the physical body, the mind, or the spirit.

Working the stress-related equivalents of demanding secular work schedules, these nonprofessional staff people need time to refresh body and spirit, lest their burden of work make them susceptible to inadequate preparation, personal burnout, and family problems.

Psychologists suggest that guilt has been the traditional force driving members to a higher level of service for the church. Some excellent service is rendered this way, but through better and proper motivation, happier relationships and improved ministries would result.

These problems, existing in the Christian volunteer labor force, are not unknown in the secular world. The world of business has found it ever more difficult to increase the level of productivity and job faithfulness, even with tempting incentives. If their perks and financial awards do not awaken a sense of company loyalty, you can appreciate the problem of the volunteer force in the church, who must wait for "pie in the sky" as a reward for faithful service.

These two are constant factors—a supernatural story that needs human telling and a volunteer force to do the telling. Little wonder the vast disparity between the heavenly church "ideal" and the earthly church "real." It seems a marvel that the Lord hopes to accomplish His task of reaching the world with His gospel.

Frustration

A pastor of a large suburban church on the east coast had everything going for him, but he was frustrated. "These people really have no desire to relate to each other. They are content to sit, listen, and then pursue their own personal ambitions. I don't know how to get through to them," he said. Then he revealed a common reaction to a difficult situation. "Do you think it's time for me to look elsewhere, for people who are interested in a more vital Christianity?"

His feeling is shared by many who have felt the pulse of vibrant New Testament Christianity, compared it with the faint heartbeat of their own congregations, and wondered what has turned the body of Christ into a near corpse. That recognizable variance causes endless frustration. Many scholars suggest that this is the

reason pastorates average only four years. Young seminary graduates, unable to deal with frustration in their early ministries, are
more apt to quit the ministry during the first three years than later.

Let's examine a typical month of incidents that cry for some kind
of pastoral response:

- A leading board member loudly disagrees with a new staff
  realignment that has taken six months to design.
- A staff member causes distress among the secretaries because
  of his petulant attitude.
- The head of the coffee table ministry is appalled at the seeming
  ingratitude of the congregation.
- The kitchen crew is upset because within two years most of the
  table settings have disappeared.
- The senior pastor receives evidence that a recent wedding he
  performed was not between a man and a woman.
- An accusation of homosexual activity is leveled against two
  prospective members.
- Two more cases of dreaded breast cancer among the ladies of
  the congregation have been reported.
- A recent stewardship emphasis caused two families to stop
  attending.
- A newly-appointed chairman of a major committee died while
  on a business trip.
- It is discovered that one of the church leaders is guilty of forni-
  cation.
- A group of members are withholding their giving until the
  "board gets it all together." Interpretation: Until they do things
  our way.
- Word comes that widespread drinking is occurring at a retreat
  for young adults.
- The pastor receives a four-page letter criticizing a recent sermon.
- One of the leading musicians has embraced the charismatic
  movement.
- A board member is upset because no one from the church
  called on the visitors he brought last Sunday.
- Someone's elderly aunt was hospitalized and received no visit
  from the staff.

Every pastor could recite his own list of sad tales demonstrating the variance between the professed and the practiced. Every congregation, especially the middle-class, suburban congregation, lives behind a facade that hides life in the raw. What mortals these saints really be! The larger the church, the more numerous and complex the problems. This drama of human needs is played out against the backdrop of a pastoral heart that embraces the vision of an ideal church and the mission of God's call to preach. His frustration is heightened by several factors.

Dehumanization

No one individual has the time or the capacity to solve every problem in the church. The human psyche is incapable of dealing in detail with such a variety of demands. Failure to recognize this fact can result in breakdown, burnout, or hypocrisy (which may be the worst). No wonder some pastors become religious robots mouthing pious platitudes while longing inwardly for the elusive "better church" or the next vacation. Perhaps we have been requiring of ourselves more than God does in our efforts to live up to the expectations of the congregation. The human machine is not designed to carry such a load alone.

Unmanageable Organization

Frustration can come to a pastor when he attempts to bring efficiency out of an unmanageable organizational chaos.

Some church organizational charts are like scaffolding erected after the building is built. One pastor I know is involved with a growing church. His congregation has a large staff, so he assigned an executive pastor to direct the burgeoning ministry. When I asked the pastor to state the church's major goal for that year, he replied, "My executive pastor and I are going to sit down and try to develop some kind of philosophy for all of this."

Philosophy should *precede* organization in a church. It should lead the ministry, not lag behind it. Erratic, unguided programming will usually fail because it lacks consistency with some major purpose. If we have not formulated a Biblical approach to ministry, how can we possibly judge which ministries are good or which are not good? A philosophy of ministry is a necessity, so that goals can be set and structures put in place to express and fulfill that philoso-

phy. Only then can we avoid costly program cancellations, be-
leaguered Christian servants, and despair and disappointment.

Even a momentary period of growth cannot justify a lack of
Biblical philosophy. Unguided growth in ministry, lacking a con-
nection to a well-thought-out philosophy, will inevitably dissipate
because it will fail to sustain interest. Unrestrained growth follows
no predesigned pattern, thus weakening the host organism. Many
cancer cells are quite healthy.

If the church is not more effectively directed, its efforts will be
counterproductive to the mandate and purpose of our Lord. The
church can fail miserably if it does not use all the means the Lord
has provided for reaching the world. Lack of an effective organizational approach to express the church's unchanging mandate can
cause frustration in pulpit and pew, followed by discouragement
and failure on the part of either or both.

Lack of Emphasis on Preaching

Some ministers will secretly admit that their churches are doing
some unbiblical things, that violate their calling to the ministry.
Rare is the man who has entered the ministry without feeling
called by God to "preach the Word." He feels the call strongly, and
prays fervently that preaching might be his gift. He wants to be
good at it, and if he is, that is where he will be most productive.
But the increased demands of administration, counseling, problem
solving, and endless meetings soon destroy not only the time but
the appetite for effective Biblical ministry. His sermons lack the
impact he desires because he has not invested the time or depth of
thought that allows sparkling creativity. Interest lags in the congregation, volunteers begin to disappear, growth slows.

Recently I attended a conference in North Carolina with twenty
pastors of large churches. The format for the two-and-one-half-day
marathon session permitted us to challenge, confirm, and confess
with each other, eyeball to eyeball. We discovered that the number
one difficulty we faced was preserving study and research time
amid the increasing demands of administration. At the last session
I asked them what had been the basis of their church growth. They
all believed that growth took place because they were effective in
the pulpit. Each one sensed that, unless his battle was won to
maintain inviolate time in the study, the vitality and growth of his

congregation would suffer. They were struggling to maintain the integrity of pulpit ministry.

Dallas equipped me well for expository preaching, and I still believe that such preaching is the center of ministry. No matter what organizational innovations take place, the expository ministry of the Word must never be sacrificed. I agree with Bob Smith at Peninsula Bible Church when he describes the focal point of ministry. "Total Christian education should be our goal. . . . It's like a big burner: the expository pulpit ministry is the center of the burner, and the complementary efforts with their greater participation possibilities form the outer rings of the burner."[1]

The Need for a Biblical Philosophy of Ministry

The most common church organization is unbiblical not only because it diminishes the prophetic role, but also because it limits the ministry of the masses. If we believe in the priesthood of all believers we can find no Scriptural support for congregations of observers or audiences. Many churches, fortified by the traditional concept of ministry, and mummified by a low opinion of their own spiritual capabilities, continue to miss the blessing of an every-member ministry.

If pastors can become frustrated, it is also true for whole churches. They wonder what they can do to survive. There is a price to pay for embracing a traditional or unbiblical approach to ministry. People grow listless, apathetic, to the point of suffering spiritual atrophy, when they are not involved in a challenging ministry. Scriptures meant for warriors lose their meaning when they are addressed to those on inactive duty.

A close corollary to apathy is a worsening critical nature. It is easy for those not directly involved in ministering to engage in criticism of those who are, perhaps thereby hoping to excuse themselves for noninvolvement. A South Jersey pastor moved into a church crisis which had reached near split proportions. Criticism, angry charges, and unloving epithets were hurled with such venom that most of the board members had resigned. But after three years of his leadership the original wound in the body was only a barely recognizable scar. The healing had been accomplished as this man led his people into involvement in ministry to the extent they had little time to engage in fault-finding.

Christians become increasingly restless because they are denied the opportunity to serve in ministry even though they are equipped to serve. They may be oppressed by a traditional organizational pattern or by an overly cautious pastor, who is so insecure he is extremely hesitant to share the ministering function. Restlessness finally issues in dissatisfaction that brings loss of interest in the ministry of the local body.

When Christians become uninvolved in the work of the church, leaving their personal spiritual lives in neutral, they can become prey to those who offer them a new Christian experience. Most cults and "isms" grow at the expense of the established church, offering disgruntled members a new warmth or a new approach. Generally those who are actively engaged in ministry in the body have more of a built-in resistance to such an approach. Cults thrive where ministering has died.

Many parachurch organizations also thrive because the local church has failed to recognize and make use of gifted and enthusiastic members. The parachurch ministry becomes more appealing, offering excitement and opportunity and providing fresh outlet for using one's personal gifts.

Such problems will persist in the church that refuses to embrace a Biblical philosophy of ministry in fulfilling the mandate to reach its community. It is foolish to say and naive to hope that all these problems will disappear, but an aggressive Biblical philosophy will go a long way in helping to diminish them, encouraging the local church in its effectiveness.

What is a Biblical philosophy? It is a systematic approach to ministry based upon specific principles identified in the New Testament teaching on the body of Christ. While obvious to some, other pastors (myself included) overlooked the New Testament principles for a growing church for many years.

This book is about the discovery of those principles and an effective, developing approach to bring them to reality.

---

[1]Bob Smith, *When All Else Fails*. Waco, TX: Word Books, 1974, p. 58.

CHAPTER 2

Developing the Biblical Base

The church is a supernatural body endowed with supernatural abilities (gifts) to maintain its own health and growth in order to have an effective impact upon an alienated world.

The Old Testament Perspective

Contemporary evangelical churches more often reflect Old Testament thinking rather than New Testament perspectives. Consider the three basics in Old Testament structure.

The Temple
The temple signified the localized presence of God. This building was holy and central to the thinking of the Old Testament Jew.

But we are too building-oriented, believing not only that the work of God is localized in a structure, but that there is something holy about that structure. We betray ourselves by describing our Sunday practice as "going to church," even though we realize how theologically erroneous such a statement is.

Our place of worship is described as the "sanctuary." Elders and deacons still get upset about teenagers disregarding the "house of God." I smile when I think of the horror on the faces of some older Christians when they witness someone smoking "on the church steps." It is not the health issue that upsets them, but the thought that such sacrilege is taking place near the holy house of God. So deeply ingrained is "sanctuary thinking" that people still grimace when I refer to our Sunday morning meeting place as the auditorium.

Temple-thinking dies hard, even among evangelicals.

The Priesthood

The priesthood was the special class (tribe) of people whose responsibility it was to serve God. These people had a particular function among God's chosen.

The reverence and expectation originally reserved for the Old Testament priesthood has, in our time, been transferred to the pastoral staff. We are seen as an exclusive group, set apart from the ordinary folk. The pastor is a professional whose traditional area of expertise is this spiritual ministry. He can counsel, preach, pray, evangelize, teach, baptize, and bury the dead. No matter who else visits the sick, gives advice, or runs the meeting, it doesn't really count unless the pastor does it.

Sacrifices

Sacrifices were offerings man made to God in order to be well-pleasing to Him. In the Old Testament they were the formal means by which the people worshiped God.

In a disturbing trend, evangelicals are becoming more and more formalistic, rationalizing their drift because of a seeming lack of "worship" among the evangelical church. I suspect this trend is more often the reflection of a sophisticated, aesthetic taste than the result of serious Bible study. History has shown us that those lacking a vital spiritual life often transfer their spiritual emphasis to forms and give those forms the transcendence of mystical meaning. Forms are not alive—the Word is! What is necessary for vital worship is an inward spiritual response to the truth (John 4).

Many of our long-established churches have a philosophical and practical affinity to Old Testament practices. Not only is this unrewarding spiritually, but it places a troublesome restraint on the distribution and the enjoyment of ministry by the people.

The New Testament Perspective

During His earthly ministry, Jesus Christ gave two great promises that have a direct bearing on our discussion.

The Spirit

One great promise concerns the Holy Spirit. During the earthly ministry of Christ the Spirit was very active, but Christ anticipated a change in the Spirit's ministry and encouraged the disciples regarding this new relationship. In John 14:17 two prepositions anticipate the change. Speaking of the Holy Spirit, Jesus said, "You know Him [the Spirit of truth] because He abides *with* you, and will be *in* you."

Elsewhere John explained how and why this change would take place. Jesus said, "He who believes in Me, as the Scripture said, 'From his innermost being shall flow rivers of living water'" (John 7:38). Many years later, as John wrote his Gospel, he explained what Jesus meant by "rivers of living water." John wrote, "He spoke of the Spirit, whom those who believed in Him were to receive; for the Spirit was not yet given, because Jesus was not yet glorified" (John 7:39). The coming of the Spirit was seen to be in the future. The Holy Spirit had not yet come to individual Christians because somehow that new relationship was linked to the death and resurrection of Jesus Christ.

Peter delivered his first sermon on the day of Pentecost after the arrival of the Holy Spirit, whose coming caused much questioning. In Acts 2:33 Peter showed he understood the link between the coming of the Holy Spirit and the glorification of Christ. "Therefore, having been exalted to the right hand of God, and having received from the Father the promise of the Holy Spirit, He has poured forth this which you both see and hear." The glorification of Jesus Christ was the key to the coming of the Holy Spirit.

Two remarkable and significant differences are apparent between the Old Testament and the New Testament ministry of the Spirit. First, after Pentecost the Holy Spirit would dwell in every believer individually, not just a special few fitted for prophetic work or priestly service. Peter said, "You shall receive the gift of the Holy Spirit. For the promise is for you and your children, and for all who are far off, as many as the Lord our God shall call to Himself" (Acts 2:38, 39).

Second, the Spirit of God would be a permanent indweller. That was not so in the Old Testament. Saul had the Spirit removed from him (1 Samuel 16:14). David realized that this removal could happen and so prayed that the Holy Spirit would not be taken from him (Psalm 51:11). But the believer has the Holy Spirit as a permanent possession. In fact, the New Testament insists that if someone does not possess the Holy Spirit then he really isn't a Christian (Romans 8:5). The Holy Spirit's presence is a pledge or an earnest of our inheritance. We are sealed in the Holy Spirit (Ephesians 1:13, 14).

The finished work of Christ has made us fit vessels for the indwelling of the presence of God through the Holy Spirit. The adjective most used to describe the character of the Spirit is *holy*. How could such a Holy One dwell in an uncleansed vessel? But Jesus Christ came and, by His death, resurrection, and ascension, completely and forever removed the believer's sin and made him acceptable to a holy God. The believer stands forever justified before Him. God's verdict is that each believing sinner is now righteous before Him through the death of Christ. Having been thus permanently cleansed, we are now fit residence (temples) for the Holy One, the third person of the Godhead.

Moses's completion of the tabernacle recorded in Exodus 40 is a dramatic illustration. Moses did the anointing and cleansing, set the tabernacle curtains and the hangings, burned the incense, and offered the offerings. Only then, when Moses had finished, did the eternal God of the universe come to dwell in that tent. "Thus Moses finished the work. Then the cloud covered the tent of meeting, and the glory of the Lord filled the tabernacle" (Exodus 40:33, 34). God dwelt in a tent made of animal skins.

So it is with the church. Jesus Christ finished the work and was glorified. Then, and only then, did the glory of the Lord, in the person of the Holy Spirit, come and fill the tent—our tent. No wonder Paul writes to the Corinthians that our bodies are no longer considered merely bodies. "Do you not know that your body is a temple of the Holy Spirit who is in you, whom you have from God?" (1 Corinthians 6:19) A great promise is now fulfilled. The Holy Spirit is no longer just *with* us, He is *in* us. This was made possible because of the finished work of Christ, which had so cleansed the believing sinner that he has become a fit dwelling place for the Holy Spirit.

The Church

Jesus made another promise to the disciples: "I will build My church" (Matthew 16:18).

At the time of the promise the church was wholly in the future. The verb is, "I will build." God, up to that time, had used the nation of Israel as a channel and instrument through which He communicated with the world. The law, the prophets, and even the Messiah came through that earthly channel. But a change was coming.

The church was to be a supernatural organism. Membership in the nation of Israel was by birth and circumcision. The church, however, would be the result of His initiative and the process of building. The church would be different than a nation. It would be a group of "called-out ones" *(ekklesia)*.

Like the promise of the Holy Spirit, the promise to build His church was fulfilled on the day of Pentecost. Jesus said that on that day, "You shall be baptized with the Holy Spirit" (Acts 1:5). He referred to John's baptism of water, which identified repentant sinners with John's message in time. Now a different baptism was to take place, which would create a whole new identification and union. John was a human being, and as such he could only baptize with a substance he could control at will—water. John could never baptize with the Holy Spirit, because no human being could have sovereign control over God. The very fact that Jesus Christ could baptize with the Holy Spirit is an evidence of His deity (John 1:33).

The repercussions of that fact are far-reaching. That baptism places us in the body of Christ.

Paul, while referring to the oneness of the body, discusses how it was achieved. "For by one Spirit were we all baptized into one body" (1 Corinthians 12:13). The baptizing work of the Holy Spirit, which places the Christian within the body of Christ, the church, fulfills both promises—bestowing the Holy Spirit and bringing the church into existence. These two great promises of change, delivered during the earthly ministry of Christ, awaited fulfillment until He was seated at His Father's right hand. The promise of the new ministry of the Spirit and the promise of the new organism called the church were both fulfilled on the same day, at the same time.

Why Change Was Necessary

An instructive parallel exists between the person of Christ and the church. Jesus Christ was the Word who became flesh and dwelt among us, and we beheld His glory (John 1:14). Jesus Christ communicated the nature and character of God. His life was a demonstration of what God is like and what He is all about. Jesus came not only to demonstrate but to proclaim the truth of God and accomplish His will (John 17:6-8). That demonstration and proclamation culminated in the cross and the resurrection. There God spoke supremely through His Son (Hebrews 1:2). The Word had become flesh—that was the first incarnation. The second person of the Godhead, the Son, became flesh.

Now, since the Holy Spirit has arrived, a second incarnation has taken place. The church is indwelt by Him for the identical purpose of communicating God. Jesus Christ has ascended to Heaven, but He has not left the earth without the light of witness.

The church, the body of Christ, is to demonstrate the nature and character of God. Peter put it this way, "You are ... a people for God's own possession, that you may proclaim the excellencies of Him who called you out of darkness into His marvelous light" (1 Peter 2:9). The transformed Christian life should "prove what the will of God is, that which is good and acceptable and perfect" (Romans 12:2).

That demonstration—revelation—is helpful only if the church is growing and maturing. Since the revelation of the nature and character of God is beyond all human ability, we as fallen but redeemed creatures need the supernatural provision of the Holy Spirit to demonstrate the character of God. The qualities of God as listed in Galatians 5:22, 23 (love, joy, peace, patience, kindness, goodness, faithfulness, gentleness, self-control) can be provided only by the life-giving quality of the Holy Spirit. A life that has a resemblance to God can only be the product of the "fruit of the Spirit."

The church is not only called to *be* something, but to *do* something. Even before the great truths of the church life were taught in Ephesians, Philippians, and Colossians, the early Christians were told exactly what they were to do. The gospels and the first chapter of Acts record the commission of Jesus Christ to proclaim the good news. With that proclamation, the early Christians were to beseech humanity to be reconciled unto God.

This too is a supernatural process. The world is under the power of the evil one. Man is dead in sin. To counter all the satanic lies and bring life to the dead cannot be achieved by human strength, ingenuity, or clever manipulation. This is why Jesus said it was to the disciples' advantage that He leave; if He did not, the Helper would not come. But when the Helper (the Holy Spirit) came, He would "convict the world concerning sin, righteousness and judgment" (John 16:8). The presence and power of the Holy Spirit were needed to challenge the forces of darkness that had aligned themselves with the perverse nature of humanity.

Jesus told His early disciples to wait for the promise of the Father (Acts 1:4). These were men who had heard His teaching, seen His miracles, been exposed to His loving character, and had even been eyewitnesses of the resurrection. In addition to all these benefits, they had actually been with the risen Christ listening to Him expound the things of the kingdom of God. Surely these men were ready. Had they not been fortified with "many convincing proofs"? (Acts 1:3) Yet they were not ready. Jesus said they were to wait; they were not to depart from Jerusalem until the promise of the Father came upon them. No zeal, reasoning power or emotional confidence could substitute for the Spirit's power. They were not to preach or teach without Him. If they who were eyewitnesses, beholders of the truth, could not adequately minister without the Spirit, what makes us believe we can?

The Meaning for the Church

Peter sums up the contrast in chapter two of his first letter. He had lived through the transition from the physical temple to the spiritual body of Christ and was well aware of the difference. "You also, as living stones, are being built up as a spiritual house for a holy priesthood, to offer up spiritual sacrifices acceptable to God through Jesus Christ" (1 Peter 2:5).

First there was the change in God's localized presence upon this earth. God had dwelt in a tent, then in the temple. But now God lives in a spiritual house made up of living stones built upon the cornerstone, Jesus Christ.

Second there was change in the priesthood. No longer would the priesthood consist of a special class of people from a particular tribe. It would consist of all people who believed in Jesus Christ. They were to be a holy priesthood. What a grand and glorious privilege—each believer is called upon to be a priest!

Finally, the sacrifices would no longer be some formalized, customized kind that seemed to have more merit in themselves than in the offerer. The new sacrifices were to be "spiritual" sacrifices— sacrifices of praise, thanksgiving, and stewardship.

Since God has made such a remarkable change, Christian organizations should reflect that change. Any organizational proposal that might hinder the every-member supernatural ministry should be seriously questioned or jettisoned. If an organizational structure focuses on a ministry in a central place, it might be more reflective of Old Testament thinking than New. If an organizational structure places ministry in the hands of a few educated professionals rather than distributing that ministry among all the believers, who are the real priests, then we may be trying to carry new wine in old wineskins. If an organization does not recognize the significance of every believer's ministry, knowing that actions and deeds are no longer just that but actually spiritual sacrifices, then it needs to be updated, upgraded and expressive of a truth so obvious in the New Testament writings. Organization should not only express a philosophy, it should expedite ministry.

God's promises heralded a radical change in the way God deals with humanity! He has called a new supernatural body, the church, into existence to have a supernatural ministry in a world

darkened by and under the control of an evil, supernatural presence. To resort to anything less than that supernatural provision is to opt for ineffectiveness and death. The church, taught about its radical role and liberated from traditional organizational trappings, can indeed have an influence against which "not even the gates of hell can prevail."

This grand and glorious calling could not have been devised by man, who has proven that his mind cannot solve the problems his own nature has raised. But there is more. God expands further on how the Holy Spirit achieves this through the body.

CHAPTER 3

Defining
the Task

The church is a supernatural body equipped with the Holy Spirit to achieve the twofold divine mission to demonstrate the character of God and declare the truth of God.

The definition of that task has a significant effect upon many church situations and the structure that evolves within a congregation. We should allow a church to grow in such a way that it becomes a healthy, effective instrument for world evangelism. Actually, this thesis is simply a restatement of an important New Testament passage on the design of the church and its implications for the task of evangelization. That passage is Ephesians 4:1-32. The basic ingredients of the passage should not only be at the heart of every local pastor, but should be taught to congregations and reaffirmed constantly to arrest any drift toward decay.

A simple statement will help summarize the content of the chapter. *Unity coexists with diversity to foster maturity and eventually an impact on the world in which we live.*

Our purpose is not to give a detailed exposition of the passage but to pick up those highlights that help in formulating a church structure. These are the basic ingredients in organizing for outreach and growth.

A Common Unity
(verses 1-7)

Unity is something that God creates in the body. Our Lord prayed that we might be one (John 17). "We are all baptized into one body," Paul says in 1 Corinthians 12:13. This sovereign act of God removes us from the race of Adam and places us in the race of the second Adam, Christ (Romans 5:12-21).

Even though we cannot create that unity, we can certainly disturb the enjoyment of it. Scripture teaches and history confirms that there can be severe ruptures in the body of Christ. That is why four qualities of life are taught in Ephesians 4:2. If these four virtues are constantly present within the body—humility, gentleness, patience, and showing forbearance to one another in love—then unity would be maintained. The same virtues are exalted in Paul's letter to the Philippians. Concerned about unity among believers, he admonished them to have "the same mind, maintaining the same love, united in spirit, intent on one purpose. Do nothing from selfishness or empty conceit, but with humility of mind let each one of you regard one another as more important than himself" (Philippians 2:2, 3). The unity created by God is maintained by the proper Christian attitudes.

So we will not be confused, Paul spells out what unity is. He says a sevenfold unity is enjoyed by all believers, and that should be enough to keep us together. "There is one body and one spirit, just as also you were called in one hope of your calling; one Lord, one faith, one baptism, one God and Father of all who is over all and through all and in all" (Ephesians 4:4-6). But this unity created by God will not be enjoyed unless there is the desire and the effort to maintain it, so Paul asks them to be "diligent to preserve the unity of the Spirit in the bond of peace" (Ephesians 4:3). The unity we enjoy is based upon the things we have in common. It can be disturbed and disrupted by a failure to maintain the correct attitude or the diligence to preserve it.

Unity is not just for unity's sake, as though there was something special in merely possessing unity. As the Ephesians passage unfolds, a reason for unity is given: maturity is not possible unless we are exposed to one another's gifts and ministries. We must be together in order to benefit from one another. Spiritual gifts cannot be exercised at a distance (except perhaps by electronic preaching, which is a poor substitute for face-to-face encounter).

When disruption takes place, two problems immediately surface. First, I am cut off from the gifts and ministry of others, whom I desperately need in order to become the person God wants me to be. Second, I deprive the other members of the body of the gifts God has given me, limiting the progress of maturity.

Perhaps I'm being too idealistic, but in my 15 years of ministry at Jacksonville Chapel I have not seen one rupture (a person leaving the fellowship) that could not have been solved by Biblical methods. The reason God has established an eldership in each local congregation is so they can lead the members under their authority in the path of ministry and unity. When people have left the church over the years because of some problem, they usually have not come before the elders, stated their case, and submitted to the elders' decision, which I believe to be a proper procedure advocated by Scripture, but avoided by most evangelical Christians. Evangelicals seem to be paranoid about authority, albeit with good historical reason. One should not despise Biblical authority properly instituted in a local congregation (Hebrews 13:17).

Unity has been established by God for a purpose. Maturity and evangelism are not possible without it. If a congregation treats unity lightly, it fails to recognize the full intent of God in placing us together in this body.

A Designed Diversity
(verses 8-12)

Unity does not mean uniformity. Christians are not the product of a heavenly assembly line. The church of Jesus Christ has a designed diversity within its unity. "But to each one of us grace was given according to the measure of Christ's gift" (verse 7).

Three important facts can be gathered from this verse.

First, each one of us has received a gift by the grace of Christ. None is exempt. None is excluded. Second, like salvation, this gift of grace is something we do not deserve or merit. No one is worthy to receive it. Third, what we have received comes from the measure of Christ. Each of us has what Jesus Christ decides we should have. Paul puts it another way in 1 Corinthians 12:11—"But one and the same Spirit works all these things, distributing to each one individually just as He wills."

These gifts come to us because of the victory of Christ. Even though Ephesians 4:8-10 seems hard to understand, the simple message is that Jesus Christ has won a great victory, and as a victor, He shares the blessings of His victory with His people. His gifts are part of the wealth He has gained by the victory. The victor distributes them as He wills.

As the discussion of gifts progresses, it changes its emphasis. Verse 7 emphasized "each one," but now the discussion deals with "some," as in verse 11. Out of the pool of gifted people, some have distinct functions and are deemed leaders in the body. Four times the word "some" is repeated to designate particularly gifted functions within the body.

It is not my purpose to discuss which gifts were intended only for that time, but to define one gift that obviously remains—the pastor-teacher gift, because of its significant place in the body of Christ.

The Pastor's Role

The word used to describe the ministry of the pastor-teacher is *katartidzo,* a descriptive and fascinating word used in the New Testament to describe various actions.

Mark 1:19. When Jesus called James and John they were *"mending"* their nets. These nets had been broken in use and, to be usable again, had to be repaired. The saints have been broken in use and can be repaired by the pastor-teacher's efforts.

Luke 6:40; Romans 9:22; Hebrews 11:3. The pupil, when "prepared," would be like his teacher (Luke 6:40). Vessels were "fitted" for destruction (Romans 9:22). The worlds were "equipped" by the

Word of God (Hebrews 11:3). This corresponds to the ancient secular use in which a guest room was furnished or ship was outfitted or equipped for a voyage. The idea is the proper outfitting for its function. This is where the NASB gets its rendering, "equipping."

Galatians 6:1. Paul writes that if any be overtaken in a fault that those who are spiritual should "*restore* such a one." The same word is used of restorative action. The ancients used it as a medical term for the setting or mending of bones.

There is hardly more than a shade of difference between the meanings. The process of *katartidzo* is to "fit" someone for a function, which means to equip or restore them in some manner. What a meaningful picture of a pastor's ministry! It would seem, then, that a pastor-teacher's ministry would have a great deal more meaning to those who are active and bruised in service.

This may explain why some Christians are unresponsive to the preached Word, no matter how powerful and penetrating it is. They simply have no need for it. They are not active in the Lord's work; they have no holes that need mending, no challenges that must be answered by divine truth, have no broken bones that need the soothing care of the Word of God. Every pastor is amazed how some will leave the service blessed, weeping, touched, while others are impenetrable, unmoved. Perhaps this is a partial answer.

Attention should be called to the change of preposition in Ephesians 4:12, although the English text does not highlight it. When describing the pastor's role, it was for (*pros*) the fitting of the saints. There follow two prepositional phrases, both introduced by *eis.* The pastor's gift existed for (*pros*) the fitting of the saints for (*eis*) the work of service to (*eis*) the building up of the body of Christ. I believe these changes to be significant; in fact so much so that a proper understanding of them will shatter the traditional concept of the pastor and church life.

The pastor's role is to *equip the saints* for the work of service and the building up of the body of Christ. These last two ministries, the work of service and the building up of the body, have historically been associated with and assigned to professional clergymen. This attitude has probably contributed to the crippling of the body of Christ more than any other misunderstanding. Because the pastor has not rightly understood his role, he has accepted responsibilities that really were not his, thereby diminishing his impact and robbing the average member of the body of Christ of that which God has given him. We have ineffective congregations because we have disillusioned pastors and disinterested people. The answer to lethargy in the local church congregation is not so much revival (which usually settles back into the same old pattern) but rearrangement. When pastor and people take seriously their God-given and God-designed responsibilities, then vitality is soon to follow.

The People's Role

Blessed are the people whose pastor has the perspective of Ephesians 4:11, 12, because it fosters two important ideas.

The work of the ministry. Ministry is not a game; it is work. People in ministry get battered and bruised. The work of ministry includes evangelization, care, administration, and much more. It means getting bored listening to people with endless problems. It means observing firsthand the heartbreak of someone who showed much spiritual promise going down the spiritual "tubes." It means playing peacemaker among a leadership who have brought too much ego into the ministry. The list goes on and on. People doing the work of ministry quickly develop a deep respect and love for their pastor. They no longer consider him a useless anachronism left from colonial times. To them he becomes someone whose words and instructions are needed because the battle is intense and personal.

The building up of the body of Christ. People who realize that the health of the body depends on their ministry have a different perspective than those who see the body only as a collection of people who are fair game for unending criticism and gossip. Many can tear down the body; they've had long experience at it and, sometimes, effective examples. When the church is no longer "their church," "his church," or "your church," but "my church," then a concern develops that should parallel that of the pastor. I could no longer abandon the body any more than I could abandon my own children. The church's welfare, health and growth become my concern. I am trained and equipped for building up the church.

The responsibility of the people could be represented this way:

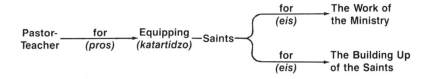

Each person is gifted supernaturally, but some are gifted with the equipping gifts to outfit the saints to fulfill their function of working and building up the kingdom of God.

A Growing Maturity
(verses 13-16)

Ephesians 4:13-16 teaches us that when this process is fully operational, the pastor and the people fulfilling their respective roles, then growth takes place. The end result is best described as "maturity." The word "mature" is *telios,* a derivative of the term *telos,* meaning "a designed end." The concept is enlarged by the phrase, "To the measure of the stature which belongs to the fulness of Christ (Ephesians 4:13). God is making us into the image of Christ—the people He designed us to be.

The Ephesians passage suggests various elements of maturity.

Unity. "Until we all attain to the unity of the faith." That unity is spelled out in Ephesians 4:4-6—the ability to be together and stay together in spite of differences in gifts, in spite of differences in the growth process, in spite of differences in culture or race. We must be together in order to benefit from the mutual exchange of gifts.

Stability. Another aspect of maturity is stability. One area of stability is negative, and it means being *persistent* in the face of error. Another is positive—being *productive* in the face of error. "We are no longer to be children, tossed here and there by waves, and carried about by every wind of doctrine, by the trickery of men, by craftiness and deceitful scheming" (v. 14). Early in its history false teaching and doctrine threatened the church. Almost every New Testament letter was written to deal with some doctrinal deviation that threatened to diminish the light that God had established. Maturity demanded that Christians stand against the errors that came upon the early church scene. Things haven't changed. Every generation of Christians has faced challenges from cults and "isms." The faithful remained on course amidst the waves because men and women, learned in the Word of God, kept a steady hand on the helm. Stability is a necessity for survival.

But the church is called upon not only to survive, but to succeed. We cannot wait until optimum conditions prevail. We cannot wait until we have a life free of problems before we serve God; the church cannot wait until all its enemies lie in the dust before going forward. Like Nehemiah we labor with a sword in one hand, a trowel in the other.

The positive aspect of stability is to "speak the truth in love." That is how the church succeeds. The church's environment will remain hostile, but it will not deter the advancement of the kingdom. Not everyone will believe, but many will. The church is not intimidated by clashing swords or fiery darts because it realizes that any man is a pushover for God. Thus it continues to remain firm against the onslaught, faithful to the task.

Harmony. A third aspect of maturity is given in verse 16. "The whole body, being fitted and held together by that which every joint supplies, according to the proper working of each individual part, causes the growth of the body for the building up of itself in love."

Paul is fond of the analogy of the human body as an example and even a definition of the church. Despite differences, the individual parts work in synchronization with each other, not at odds with each other. What a wonderful thing to behold—a church of many diverse talents all being allowed to work together, yet each fulfilling its own individual role. No part of the body ought to think that it is unnecessary (1 Corinthians 12:15, 16); no part should think that it has no need for the others (1 Corinthians 12:21). God has given each one of us a different genetic makeup, different cultural and family background, and different combinations of gifts. Only when we truly recognize our God-designed uniqueness will we ever work as the body of Christ should.

Our diagram could be enlarged in this manner:

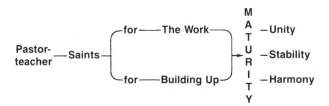

An Effective Ministry (verses 17-32)

What happens when this process is in good working order? The pastor-teacher equips the saints for the work of ministry, which contributes to the maturity of the church. The transformed body can then present to the world an alternative message and an alternative lifestyle. That is the New Testament means of evangelism. That's why Paul writes, "This I say therefore, and affirm together with the Lord, that you walk no longer just as the Gentiles also walk" (v. 17). Then follows a catalog of the unbelieving lifestyle, a lifestyle of futility, irrationality, lust, selfishness, greed, etc. The body of Christ, made up of changing, transformed individuals, confronts this world with a radical difference.

Perhaps the church has ceased to be effective in many segments of society because it has ceased to confront them with a different lifestyle. I sincerely believe that the world has nothing to match that group of people who are "growing up" in Christ. A maturing Christian body is a wonder to behold. I believe that the greatest lie Satan has ever perpetrated on this world is that God is a drag, that the Christian life is boring, unattractive, and dull. Perhaps there have been some who unwittingly have supported that lie by their own lifestyles, but they were certainly not fulfilling God's design. We are transformed so that we can contradict the lie by showing that God's will is good, acceptable and perfect (Romans 12:2). The lifestyle that God gives is exciting. Nothing can match it.

We present to this world a new life and a new message. That message, spelled out in Ephesians 4:17-32, is possible because of the God-designed maturing process that comes about when the pastor fulfills his role and the saints accept their responsibility. A transformed, effective, mature life will then confront the world, which so desperately needs it.

Once this process is operative in a local assembly, I believe it will replace reluctance with revitalization. God's people will have a different reason for serving other than guilt and obligation.

Appreciation of these basic facts about the nature and meaning of gifts will help motivate more Christians for ministry and correct some of the traditional abuses that exist in a local church. The next chapters explore some of the practical outworking of a gifted ministry.

CHAPTER 4

Gifts for Ministry

Throughout some 30 years of ministry I have observed several types of Christians within the body of Christ.

First, there is the *supersaint*. He or she teaches a Bible class, attends missionary meetings, serves on the board and several committees, serves Communion, enrolls in the Evangelism Explosion program and serves as a leader in the Christian Service Brigade. His spirituality consists of perpetual motion. Folks like him always make up a small percentage of the church. He is a prime candidate for spiritual burnout, which often manifests itself in a critical spirit and a short fuse.

The supersaint could not exist without the presence of several other kinds of saints in the body. He must be accompanied, and always is, by the *sleeping saint*—present in the body but absent in involvement. He is synonymous with the "worshiping wart," one who draws nourishment from the body but provides no function but irritation.

Another individual in the body might be termed the *scared saint*. He finds himself in his present ministry because he was afraid to say no—he could not bear to disappoint the pastor or trigger some personally imposed guilt mechanism. At the first appearance of disagreement he will disappear, blaming his abandonment of ministry on the failure of others.

Another is called the *sorry saint*. This Christian is usually shy and withdrawn and can be easily overlooked by an aggressive, growing congregation. He perceives the church to be unfriendly, uninterested in him and, lacking personal initiative, he interprets his problems as the failure of the church. His needs are not met and his gifts unused.

Another, closely resembling the above, is what I call the *scarred saint*. These are usually former supersaints who gave much without being recognized or affirmed; perhaps they were even misunderstood. They attend church but usually sit in the back, not wanting to risk involvement again.

Finally, there is the *starter saint*, a brand-new Christian in the Lord, overflowing with enthusiasm, wishing to be at every meeting, volunteering for every job. Watch carefully—the starter saint can easily change into a supersaint too soon and be a prime candidate for collapse.

What Is Wrong?

Has God impoverished His body? Has He neglected to plan for an effective ministry? Our study of Ephesians 4 shows us that God has greatly enriched the body. Charles Spurgeon once told about visiting an elderly woman in a home for the poor. Upon the wall of her little room she had hung a framed piece of paper with some writing on it. The woman explained that it had been given to her by an aged man for whom she had cared many years, and she had kept it as a memento. Spurgeon examined it and asked the woman if he could have it for a day or two.

The woman agreed, and Spurgeon took it to the bank. When the officers examined it, they said, "We've been wondering to whom the old gentleman left his money." The paper turned out to be a will, leaving all the man's money to the poor woman. She had lived in poverty for many years, never realizing all of that wealth was at her disposal.

In the same manner the church has been enriched by Christ, but it has limped along, saddled by a philosophy and restricted by a tradition that places most of the ministry in the hands of a few. What power could be unleashed if the wealth were not only realized, but spent!

Can we accuse God of being a poor planner, granting the privilege of ministry to a select few and ignoring the vast numbers of the body of Christ? If we observe God's work in the natural world, we find incredible organization at every turn. If we enter the spiritual world of angels, we can see mighty beings following His will and design. The prophetic picture informs us that redeemed humanity from every age delight to do His will. Jesus Christ himself, the essence of perfection, wisdom, and power, readily submitted to the will of God.

When we observe God's design we discover a simple principle for our own lives: *I must be available to be usable.* All of God's enrichment and design of the body of Christ remains ineffective if we are not available. This principle can be seen in Paul's letter to the Romans, chapter twelve. For eleven chapters Paul has told us what God has accomplished for us in Jesus Christ. Now he speaks to us about the life and service of believers. Verses 1 and 2 talk about availability and verses 3-8 talk about spiritual gifts and usability. After what Christ has accomplished for us, the Christian should make himself available to God. "Therefore . . . present your bodies a living and holy sacrifice."

The body is a vehicle of action. The mind needs the body to carry out its directives. If the brain receives a hunger message from the stomach, the brain in turn instructs the body to do something about it. My body cannot say to my brain, "I'm sorry, I have other things to do," or "I can't get involved," or "I'm not available right now." If this should happen in real life, it is a severe problem caused by a stroke, disease, or paralysis. God wishes to demonstrate His will to the world. He needs a body to do so. Even Jesus Christ said, "A body you prepared for me." That one is resurrected and gone. God looks for another—yours and mine!

The Exciting Work of God

Paul went on to say that the will of God is good, acceptable, and perfect, and that it is the Christian's task to demonstrate this fact. Satan has deceived us into accepting a lifestyle that promises much and delivers nothing. Simone Weil said, "Nothing is so beautiful, nothing is so continually fresh and surprising, so full of sweet and perpetual ecstasy as the good; no desert is so dreary and monotonous and boring as evil. But with fantasy it's the other way around. Fictional good is boring and flat while fictional evil is varied, intriguing, attractive and full of charm." Such is Satan's lie.

My father was a musician in Philadelphia. His work was seasonal. When the society leaders went to spend their summers at the New Jersey shore, all the musicians and bands would go as well, so I looked forward to that every summer. One summer my dad told us he could not find work at the shore, so we would have to spend the summer in Philadelphia. I vividly remember sitting out on our front steps, sad and dejected, with shattered hope. Then I heard the phone ring inside. After my mother answered it, she ran out and hugged me, saying, "Dad found a job in Atlantic City. Pack your bags—we're on our way!" What a tremendous change! I would not have to waste my life that summer on the streets of Philadelphia.

Similarly, the Christian does not have to look forward to a life of drudgery and boredom. God says that we can be involved in the most wonderful work ever—serving Him and the body of Christ. He has equipped us with supernatural gifts that are absolutely necessary to that body. We can change one another. Isn't it great to be involved?

The work of God becomes exciting for us because of the implications that emerge from Ephesians 4.

I Have Great Dignity

Christianity calls for serving and loving others. That is not possible without a growing, positive, Biblical self-image, a prerequisite for enjoyable Christian service.

Jesus gave us a remarkable living parable in John 13. After supper He took a towel and girded himself and began to wash the disciples' feet. Assuming the role of a servant was hardly possible

for the disciples at the time, because they were arguing about who among them would be the greatest (Luke 22:24). With this concern on their minds they would hardly do anything that would risk their position in the eyes of others.

Why did Jesus wash their feet? The answer is found in John 13:3. Jesus knew "that the Father had given all things into His hands, and that He had come forth from God, and was going back to God." He knew He was exalted and dignified in the eyes of God. It did not matter that Judas would betray Him, the Romans would execute Him, the religious leaders and the mob would reject and ridicule Him, or even that the disciples would abandon Him. He knew who He was. His dignity was intact because it was granted to Him by God. Taking a towel and serving someone else would never threaten it.

The great things we hold in common as Christians were spelled out in Ephesians 4:4-6. Actually, these verses are a condensed summary of the first three chapters that explained our exalted position "in Christ." That position is graciously permanent. Therefore I am free to serve and to minister to others. I no longer have to struggle for my place in the sun. My dignity is not threatened by serving and loving others.

My childhood was not much to brag about. I was born and raised in the slums of Philadelphia. My parents never graduated from high school. I was never much of an athlete and less of a ladies' man. One day, however, someone took an interest in me and taught me how to swim competitively. I wasn't great at that, but with my knowledge of the ocean and the endurance I had built up, I became an excellent ocean swimmer. When I turned 17 I decided to try out for the dream of my life—the Ocean City Beach Patrol.

That organization was more than a job; it meant prestige, hero worship, and girls! After an intensive winter of training I showed up for the big test. Thirty-seven of the top swimmers of Philadelphia and New Jersey were there. The captain informed us that there were eight jobs open. It was a rough day, right after a northeaster, but I swam my heart out and finished sixth. The day they handed me my lifeguard jacket and uniform was the proudest day of my young life. I belonged to something special.

All that is gone now; the old jacket now hangs faded in my garage, just as every worldly treasure fades. All treasures but one.

I belong to the most important group on earth, Heaven, and history—the church, the body of Christ, the redeemed of God under the headship of Christ. That same dignity and feeling is with me now. I belong to something very special.

The church may not look like something very special. We are ridiculed, made the brunt of TV jokes, and held up for scorn on the talk shows, but that doesn't matter. What really counts is what we know to be true.

Moses looked out of the palace window at some dirty, mud-caked Hebrew slaves. Then he looked at his own royal finery, the treasury of Egypt, and his destiny (possibly becoming Pharaoh of the greatest nation of ancient times). Then he made a choice. He chose the ridiculed, the reproached. Why? Because they were the people of God. That is where the action was. What a glorious place to invest one's life!

God doesn't ask us just to help in a Sunday-school class; He asks us to serve the body of Christ. He does not ask us just to baby-sit in the nursery, but to serve the body of Christ. He doesn't just ask us to be an usher on Sunday morning, but to serve the body of Christ.

I have great dignity, dignity that enables me to serve without being concerned that something I do will diminish me in the eyes of others.

I Have a Great Specialty

Several years ago I badly sprained my right thumb. I never realized how important that small member of my body was. I knew the wounding of that member would severely affect my ability to write, but I didn't realize that shaving would become an impossibility. I had always taken that little right thumb for granted. Only when it wasn't usable did I see how important it really was.

Not only does the Christian possess great dignity, but a great specialty, and therefore a strategic place in the body, whether a thumb or an eye. This gift is absolutely essential for the growth and health of the body. The gifts were "victory gifts" granted by the conquest of Jesus Christ. The gifts and specialties the Christian receives are won at a great price. It would be incongruous to despise or neglect them.

One of my sons bought me a tie rack one Christmas. It had a battery-driven mechanism that revolved, and it had to be specially mounted. Because of laziness I let it sit in the box for several months. One day my son caught me off guard and said, "Dad, aren't you going to use the tie rack I gave you?" I could see the hurt in his eyes. He had bought and paid for that tie rack with his own money, and he hoped I would be pleased and use it. I put it up the next day.

The gifts that Jesus Christ has won for us are victory gifts. They are expensive. Can I really feel comfortable neglecting them?

The New Testament uses two terms to describe these gifts. One is *charismata*, which literally means "a grace thing." This means that the gift has been especially bestowed upon me and has really come from Him alone. The other word used for "gift" is *pneumatika*, which means "a spiritual thing." The term *charismata* refers to the origin of the gift; the term *pneumatika* refers to its nature. It is especially for the spiritual realm. Carnal or earthly tools cannot achieve spiritual growth or benefit; only spiritual tools can. We cannot build the supernatural body with natural tools.

These gifts were given according to the "measure of Christ." In John 3:34 we are told that Jesus Christ received the Holy Spirit without measure. He had a full complement of all the spiritual ministries. But when I receive my gift or gifts, it is according to the measure of Christ. This means that I don't have them all; 1 Corinthians 12:29, 30 says that no person has all the gifts. This distribution of gifts suggests a basic relationship among Christians: 1) *You need me.* God has given me a specialty, a tool that is necessary for the building up of your life. 2) *I need you.* I don't have all the gifts. That's why we need to maintain the unity of the body.

To absent myself from the body means not only that I will deprive you of some needed spiritual benefit, but also that I risk becoming less of the person God has designed me to be, because I cut myself off from your gifts, which benefit me.

I Have a Great Ability

So powerful is the specialty that God has granted to each member of the body of Christ that it gives them the ability to change people. The word *attain* is found in Ephesians 4:13; the term *grow up* in verse 15. The words *growth* and *building up* also appear in this context. These words all suggest good or positive change.

A great deal of money is spent on change today. Richard

Simmons says, "Are you 30 pounds overweight? I can change you." The surgeon says, "Do you have wrinkles? I can change you." Others say, "If you don't know how to dress or walk correctly, come to our school and we can change you." People make billions of dollars because they offer change. But Christians are also involved in change. Wouldn't it be wonderful if we had the power to cure blindness or cancer or lameness? Lo and behold, God offers us a ministry of change that is even greater. We can be agents of real, permanent change.

It's change that counts. There is one permanent thing on this earth. The earth itself is not permanent. The sun is not permanent, the moon is not permanent, and wealth is not permanent. People are. They are because they've been created in the image of God and they are eternal souls. They are the oniy things on earth that live forever except, of course, for the Word of God. Therefore I can invest in change that lasts forever.

One pastor was reviewing the membership rolls with his official board. Scribbled after the names of several members were the letters "FBPO." One of the board members asked the significance of those letters. "For burial purposes only!" answered the pastor. What a contrast to a thriving group of believers recognizing their own spiritual gifts and the necessity they have of ministering to one another. Inactive, lethargic people can be changed into excited contributors to the growth of the body. How? By recognizing the design that God has set up for the growth of this fantastic supernatural organism.

The church has been given wonderful gifts. It is rich because of God. Our aim is to tap those riches and live the life that God wants us to live.

The Stifling of Gifts

Six inhibitors of growth through gifts can be found in the New Testament.

Selfishness

Romans 12:1, 2 is the prelude or overture to the symphony of gifts. The possession of gifts does not automatically make us effective in the lives of other people. The Corinthian church, although extremely gifted, was divided and crippled. Romans 12:1, 2 says that we must yield to the lordship of Christ if we are going to be effective. Availability precedes usability.

The Queen of England used to summer at Balmoral Castle in Scotland. One day, as she ventured far from the castle, she saw dark clouds on the horizon and realized that rain was coming. She stopped at a small cottage to borrow an umbrella. The woman who lived there, not recognizing the Queen, was reluctant to lend her a brand-new umbrella so she gave her a castoff umbrella that had a broken rib and several holes.

The next day the lady answered a knock at the door and beheld a tall gentleman clothed in a uniform with gold braid. He said, "The Queen sent me—she asked me to thank you for the loan of your umbrella." The woman hesitated for a moment and then burst into tears, saying, "Had I known it was the Queen, I would have given her my best umbrella." When we are asked to yield, it is not just to an organization or some group; we are asked to give ourselves to God.

Exclusiveness

In 1 Corinthians 12:21 we read of a gifted member who says to the other members, "I have no need of you." Some people refuse to accept the ministry of others. They seemingly have no need. They cause twofold damage: to themselves, because they cut themselves off from the rest of the body, and to others because they deprive others of an opportunity to minister.

Uselessness

In the same context we have the opposite problem (1 Corinthians 12:15, 16). Some people believe that since they do not have the prominent gifts, they have no gifts at all. This is a direct denial of the Word of God, which says that everyone has been given a gift. But it is a persistent, harmful attitude.

A professor was leafing through a textbook and came upon a page left blank by mistake. At that moment a young man knocked on the door for a counseling appointment. As the youth settled in the chair, the professor remarked jokingly about the book in his hand. He said, "Can you believe that? Page 67 is blank. Pages 66 and 68 are printed, but 67 and where it should be is blank." The student said, "I think I know how page 67 feels."

How wonderful that God has not left anyone blank, nor has He overlooked anyone. All have been gifted by Him.

Neglect

Paul told a young leader that he was not to neglect the gift that God had given him (1 Timothy 4:14).

Ken Chafen recalled how he felt when he moved to Ft. Worth, Texas. He was disappointed with the dry north Texas landscape. However, a year later a drought-breaking rain formed a huge lake in the back of one of the engineer's dams, and everything began to get green again. When he drove outside the city of Ft. Worth, he discovered acres and acres of bluebonnets in blazing color. Before there had been nothing but dry, dead grass. He mentioned his amazement to a longtime resident of the area. The old man explained that the seeds had been lying in the soil for years just waiting for the right conditions to come.

The conditions are right for blossoming. All around are people who need you. Go ahead and blossom in blazing color.

Lack of Training

Again Paul, in addressing Timothy, says, "Kindle afresh the gift of God which is in you" (2 Timothy 1:6). Gifts become more effective with training and exposure.

Billy Graham was conducting a question and answer session with seminary students. One student, obviously tired of Greek and Hebrew, asked, "Dr. Graham, if you were my age with the world the shape that it's in, would you spend several years just in training?" Dr. Graham said, "Young man, I cannot think of a better use of your time. If you were told to go into the woods and cut down trees and were given an axe made of good steel but dull, the time spent sharpening your axe would not be considered wasted. Stay in school and sharpen your axe." All of us in the body of Christ have wonderful opportunities whereby we can sharpen our axes and become effective in the hands of God.

Immaturity

Lack of Christian character is the final element that I believe contributes to the stifling of spiritual gifts. Romans 12:8 says that when we make use of certain gifts they should be accompanied by something else—simply, heavenly oil in the machine. If one gives, he is to give with liberality. If he leads, with diligence. If he shows mercy, with cheerfulness. I've seen Christians grumble their way through the kingdom. The wheels of God are grinding, but often they are groaning, too.

Discovering the Gifts

I approached our custodian one day and told him, "One half of our home is dead electrically. The outlets and the lights won't work." He came with a voltage meter, a screwdriver, and a pair of pliers. In a short time he discovered the problem and corrected it.

Suppose I went to the physician and complained of a pain in my head, and out of his bag he took a voltage meter, a screwdriver, and pliers! I would suspect his medical expertise and begin to search the walls for some kind of diploma. You cannot discover what is causing a pain in my head with tools such as those.

How then do you discover spiritual gifts? By their very nature they are supernatural and spiritual. They are "grace things," spiritual things. If that is so, I cannot reach out and touch them, nor will I hear voices telling me that I have such and such a gift. No label will appear on my forehead identifying me as the possessor of a particular gift.

This is the great error of the charismatic movement. They seek a visible sign of an invisible gift. They look for sensory evidence of a spiritual presence. How do we know that we have the Holy Spirit, the invisible presence? They tell us that we must speak in a tongue and produce some audible, visible evidence. The charismatic offers something tangible for something intangible. If they cannot produce that visible evidence or a spectacular demonstration then we are to assume that the spiritual reality is not there. I know the Holy Spirit is in my life because the Word of God declares that He is (Romans 8:9).

How then do you go about discovering your spiritual gift? These five steps will help.

Examination

The New Testament contains lists of gifts in Romans 12, 1 Corinthians 12, and 1 Corinthians 14. The first step is to study those lists and see what God has provided you. No one has all the gifts but each has some.

Inclination

As you read those lists, you may be inclined toward certain of the gifts listed. You can identify strongly with one or two. You may already have experienced a certain joy in ministering in a particular area.

Experimentation

Get involved in a ministry that needs your particular gift. Place yourself where you can be used. Many ministries are available in most local churches; you can find tremendous outlets for your gifts. You may be surprised at what happens when you really get involved. Start with a friend or family member who takes an interest in you. You may even watch others and say to yourself, "Hey, I can do that."

Confirmation

This comes in two ways: First, you will personally be blessed in the ministry of your gift. You will be excited about your ministry and the contribution that you are making to others. It will "ring your chimes." Second, others will tell you that they have been encouraged by your ministry. They will have been helped by the use of your gifts. If the goal of the ministry of gifts is to edify and equip, then you have a confirmation of the gift you have been using when people are experiencing that edification and training.

Always be ready to give and receive encouragement from others. In this way others are confirmed in the possession of their gifts.

Education

The *use* of the gifts can be developed by training. The *gift* itself cannot be developed—the gift that comes from God does not need to be improved. The vehicle or instrument through which it operates (which means you and me) can be fine-tuned. It is the same with the presence of the Holy Spirit of God. Growth in spiritual life

does not mean that He is improving, but that I, the instrument or vehicle through which He operates, am becoming better adapted to Him. The scalpel is a tool used in surgery. What a big difference if I wield it or the doctor wields it! Training and experience makes a great difference.

Robert Frost was one of America's greatest poets. I was surprised to discover that he was not as much a scholar as he was a farmer and teacher. His poetry was so effective that he was asked to read during Kennedy's inauguration. I wondered what it is that makes a man of such humble beginnings produce and use such a tremendous gift. Perhaps the answer is to be found in one of his famous poems. In *Stopping By the Woods on a Snowy Evening,* he said, "There are promises to keep / and miles to go before I sleep." He committed himself to a course and continued it with determination to the finish. The gifts God has given us require a commitment to exercise them to the finish until He calls us home.

The body of Christ, richly endowed by the victorious Savior, has all that is necessary to carry out an effective ministry here on earth. Having understood this, church leadership must not impose any restriction or archaic organizational structure that will not allow the church the freedom to fulfill its God-designed function. Organization itself is not restrictive, but wrong organization can stifle outreach and growth.

CHAPTER 5

The Place
of the
Pulpit

Even though I have thus far advocated restructuring the organization apparatus of the church to reflect the New Testament teachings on the body of Christ, I do not believe that this alone will suffice. No structure can ever supplant the ministry of the Word in the local church. Thus I call attention to the place of the pulpit.

In recent years there has been a healthy and welcome evidence of church growth. Many books and reports have studied, analyzed, and measured burgeoning congregations, trying to understand and glean reproducible principles of growth. The creative worship techniques of David Mains's Circle Church, Ray Stedman's Body Life concepts, the Coral Ridge Evangelism Explosion program, and even Jerry Falwell's bus ministry all generated excitement and interest. Sermons, magazines, books, pamphlets, and films inundated us with encouragement and inspiration.

This kind of emphasis was long overdue. It had a needed, galvanizing effect on stagnant churches. However, it did not include enough of an emphasis upon the pulpit as a factor in church growth.

The Problem

An Assessment

Each of the churches referred to above had strong, effective pulpits. Each of the pastors is not only a student of Scripture, but also dedicated to effective communication. That did not seem to surface in the appraisal of their particular growth situations.

Articles having to do with successful churches and pastors either ignored or gave scant reference to the effective communicating pulpit. In *The Pastor's Church Handbook*, Ken Parker[1] contributed an article entitled "Seven Characteristics of a Growing Church" Only once did he mention the educational ministry, and even then he did not emphasize the pulpit. In the same book, Robert Schuller[2] talks about "Three Characteristics of a Successful Pastor." He lists the pastor as a dreamer (thinking ahead), a goal-setter, and one who will pay the cost to get the job done. Not once does he mention his role as an effective communicator. Charles Mylander[3] contributes his perspective in an article, "How to Build High Morale in Your Church." What he says is excellent. He mentions a sense of expectancy, good experiences, and God-given achievement. But again, there is no mention whatsoever of the pulpit. Even when the pulpit is mentioned in church growth studies, it is not considered a significant factor.

Many consider the pulpit an insignificant factor in church growth. Dr. Win Arn says, in an article dealing with the selection of a pastor,

> Unfortunately many churches in choosing a pastor place greatest priority on the man's ability to preach. Certainly congregations are entitled to prepared and well-delivered messages. Yet, sermon delivery represents a very small portion of the pastor's total work week. Indications are that the sermon, by itself, is a relatively minor factor in the growth of a church. How then should its pastor spend his time to have the greatest effect in church growth?[4]

He lists all the activities in which a pastor engages, including sermon preparation, and concludes, "The pastor who spends a high proportion of time visiting prospects and training laity for outreach tends to have a church with significant growth."[5]

The statistics upon which he bases this statement are from a study of four similar churches over a 10-year period.[6] The independent variable was the emphasis that each pastor placed on his activities in the church. One emphasized visiting and training, another counseling and training, another administrative duties and meetings, and another sermon preparation, studying, and reading. The one emphasizing visiting and training grew best and most rapidly. The others trailed behind, with the church emphasizing the pulpit coming in third. However, to make such conclusions on the basis of such a study, assuming that all four pulpits were the same, seems to be drawing conclusions from inadequate data and subjective appraisal.

Considered by many to be the "bible" of church growth is the book by McGavran, *Understanding Church Growth*. It is perhaps the most resourceful book on the subject in print. It should be read as a beginning text for anyone interested in church growth. However, the reader searches in vain for any discussion whatsoever of the place of the pulpit in church growth. At one point, and only one, does he refer to the magnetism of the pulpit, but he does so in a deprecating manner.

> Research should make a sharp distinction between reproducible patterns of growth and those which cannot be duplicated. Some of the most striking church growth is the work of extraordinarily gifted men — geniuses. We rejoice in these men, but do not expect to find many Dwight L. Moodys or Henry Ward Beechers in our congregations . . . for church growth which is dependent on exceptional men, one thanks God; but realizes He would probably not grant us that kind of growth. Research should look for reproducible patterns of growth possible to ordinary congregations, ordinary pastors, and ordinary missionaries.[7]

After admitting that strong, effective preaching (Moody, Beecher) does produce growth, he suggests that it is not reproducible. He says that we must find methods that can help ordinary pastors and ordinary missionaries.

While we can't all attain to the oratorical level of a Moody, a Beecher, or even a Robinson, we should never surrender a goal merely because it is unattainable. That goal provides a standard whereby we can measure our performance. The local pastor should not resign himself to less than excellence in his pulpit ministry just because he can't be an equal of a Moody or a Robinson. He can improve himself greatly. Robinson himself said, in a forum in which he discussed leadership and preaching,

> In most churches, if a pastor is an effective communicator and articulates to the congregation what that church is to be about, one of two things will happen. One, they will get rid of him – they will find that his preaching doesn't match what they want. Or, two, he will surround himself with people who share his vision and they will move forward with him.
>
> There are pastors who cannot preach, but I think a "preacher" who can't preach is like a clock that doesn't run. It's called a clock, but it isn't functioning. A preacher who can't preach has a tremendous disadvantage in most of our Protestant churches. The man who can preach has the tremendous advantage of being able to stand before his congregation and articulate to them what they ought to be doing. Before long he'll be surrounded with people who share his vision. The better a communicator he is, the stronger his position will be.[8]

After Robinson made this statement, he was challenged by one of the other men in the forum about those who really cannot do what Robinson is saying. He replied, "You'd better learn to preach! I think if you put a man in the leadership of a Protestant church and he cannot preach, he has a tremendous disadvantage."[9] Historical illustrations abound of men who thought themselves incapable of public speaking, all the way from Moses to Demosthenes – all of whom became effective communicators.

Robinson spoke of confronting some of the difficulties in communication:

> Despite the difficulty of clothing thought with words, a preacher has to do it. Unless ideas are expressed in words, we cannot understand, evaluate, or communicate them. If a preacher will not – or cannot – think himself clear so that he says what he means, he has no business in the pulpit. He is like a singer who can't sing, an actor who can't act, an accountant who can't add.[10]

An Alternative

As much as church growth experts have contributed, they have not researched the place of the pulpit in good, sustained church growth. I suspect it may have been ignored because it sometimes was assumed as obvious. It would be like excluding a section on breathing in a discussion of an individual's health. But take the obvious away and all other functions become secondary.

Although in my early ministry I emphasized the pulpit (this is what I had been trained to do at Dallas), I came to realize after about ten years that this was not my sole responsibility. The church growth books began to surface then and disturbed my perspective. I still consider the preaching of the Word as central and basic, but in addition I see the need for the distribution of the ministry and the training of laymen to accomplish that ministry. I agree with Bob Smith who, even though he has been part of the Body Life movement at Peninsula Bible Church, said,

> Total Christian education should be our goal. As one of my colleagues says, It's like a big burner: the expository pulpit ministry is the center of the burner and the complementary efforts with their greater participation possibilities form the outer rings of the burner . . . let's light up the Big Burner, not to make things hot for everyone but to warm up the saints and condition the atmosphere . . . in order to do this we must get back to the kind of expository teaching that is dedicated to lifting out and presenting the true sense of the text so that God can reach our wills through our minds.[11]

The effective pulpit is, and should be, the basis of church growth. It is the core of healthy, thriving congregations. If it is not, then this growth becomes suspect. People cannot respond to a gospel they do not hear. They cannot grow on a Word that is not ably and effectively proclaimed. The pulpit cannot and should not remain alone. It should give birth to a New Testament ministry that causes subsequent growth and outreach.

The Theology of an
Effective Pulpit

If this chapter only examined the pragmatic value of an effective pulpit, then though it may provide revealing statistics and an encouragement to preach, it really could not satisfy the heart of a Bible-loving pastor. The ultimate justification for any kind of a ministry is that it is scripturally based and exemplified. The Old Testament had its great preachers—Isaiah, Jeremiah, and others. But the New Testament also presents a justification for the preaching ministry.

The Ministry of Christ

Even a casual glance at the gospel accounts reveals that preaching was a major part of the ministry of Christ. In fact, He tried to prevent anything from interfering with it. In the first chapter of the gospel of Mark, we read the strange command to the healed leper that he was to "say nothing to anyone" (Mark 1:44). The command that Jesus gave was disobeyed, so that His movements were restricted (Mark 1:45). All of this takes on meaning when we realize His stated purpose. "Let us go somewhere else to the towns nearby, in order that I may preach there also; for that is what I came out for" (Mark 1:38). The leper's testimony restricted the preaching ministry.

Jesus was a masterful speaker. His sermons were simple yet profound, filled with illustrative material and forcefully applied to His hearers' lives. No wonder people said, "No man spoke like this man."

As part of His discipleship training, He sent His men out to preach, "and they went out and preached that men should repent" (Mark 6:12). His final command to them was to go and preach the gospel (Mark 16:15).

The Early Church

The early church continued the emphasis that Jesus Christ had started. From the birth of the church in Acts 2 to the final turning to the Gentiles in Acts 28, preaching formed a basis not only of the extension of the gospel but in the edification of believers.

The first recorded act of the Holy Spirit in the church was to enable men to preach the Word. The early church existed around the preaching and teaching of the Word. It says, "They were continually devoting themselves to the apostles' teaching" (Acts 2:42). In fact, one of the first major crises that the early church faced was the competition for the Word coming from secondary matters. They said, "It is not desirable for us to neglect the word of God in order to serve tables" (Acts 6:2).

The Word was a central factor in the burgeoning church at Antioch, when Paul and Barnabas were "teaching and preaching, with many others also, the word of the Lord" (Acts 15:35). The emphasis is seen in phrases like, "Paul began devoting himself completely to the word" (Acts 18:5). Paul understood that the Word was to be a continuous influence in the lives of the believers. To the Ephesian elders he said, "I commend you to God and to the word of His grace, which is able to build you up . . ." (Acts 20:32).

The Teaching of the Apostles

Not only by practice but by their written word, the apostles stress the centrality of preaching in the life of the church. Most instructive are the pastoral epistles, in which Paul teaches those who are to be pastors.

He mentions "instruction" against false and idle doctrines (1 Timothy 1:3-11). He lists as part of the qualification for leadership that a man should be "able to teach" (1 Timothy 3:2).

The church exists partly to be "the pillar and support of the truth" (1 Timothy 3:15).

He speaks of the "words of faith and of sound doctrine" (1 Timothy 4:6).

He encourages Timothy to "give attention to the public reading of Scripture, to exhortation and teaching" (1 Timothy 4:13).

There is to be double honor to those who work hard at preaching and teaching (1 Timothy 5:17).

Timothy was encouraged to teach and preach principles of godly living (1 Timothy 6:2).

In reference to his own ministry, Paul says he "was appointed a preacher and an apostle and a teacher" (2 Timothy 1:11).

Paul makes the supreme exhortation to Timothy when he says, "Preach the word; be ready in season and out of season; reprove, rebuke, exhort, with great patience and instruction" (2 Timothy 4:2).

The theology of preaching instructs us that the preached Word is necessary for the birth, growth, correction, and training of Christians. The pastor-teacher is necessary for equipping and outfitting the saints. We are on a firm Biblical and theological basis when we stress the centrality of the preached Word in the life of a congregation and the extension of the kingdom of God.

An Example of Growth

Whatever others have found to be the explanation of growth, at the Jacksonville Chapel growth was heavily centered on its pulpit ministry.

The Jacksonville Chapel is located in the suburbs of northern New Jersey, a highly industrialized area that is densely populated. In the past ten years our growth rate has been about 400%, nearly twice the 200% rate that church growth experts consider a high growth rate for a ten-year period. [12]

Our present average morning attendance is 1200 people. This may not seem high compared to the attendance figures of large churches in the Bible Belt, the South, or California, but our growth took place in spite of the fact that we live in a transient area. In some years we lose as many as 40 families from the Chapel's ministry. Large evangelical churches are virtually unknown here. Few churches reach 1000 in size and none, to my knowledge, numbers over 2000.

Therefore, the growth we have attained at the Jacksonville Chapel has been good, sustained, healthy growth.

The significance of preaching in the growth of the Jacksonville Chapel was confirmed by an informal survey taken among the congregation. We conducted the survey on an average Sunday morning during the worship service. Of the 1000 in attendance, we received about 900 replies. It was an excellent sampling of the attitudes of our people. We were interested in two basic questions:

1. *What caused you to attend the Chapel in the first place?* We believed that this knowledge would help us focus our attention on

the most effective future programs and not be sidetracked on non-productive efforts.

2. *What caused you to remain at the Chapel once you were here?* Again, we believed that an answer would lead us to strengthen that emphasis.

The complete survey also gave us a key to the make-up of the congregation by geography, age, and length of time at the Chapel. The figures revealed that 366 of the respondents (40% of the attenders) had been attenders of the Chapel less than three years. Of these, 113 had been there for six months or less. The next group, 3-10 years, totaled 298 people (33%). The third group, those who attended ten years or more, totaled 184 (21%). The figures reveal the newness of the congregation.

The age breakdown revealed a concentration of young adults and middle-aged people. Noticeably lacking were those over 60 years of age. This group totaled only 64 people (7% of the congregation). The strong concentration of young adults and middle-aged people portrayed a healthy situation.

Though what caused people to first attend the Chapel is interesting, what is really important is what caused people to remain. We listed all the basic reasons that we had heard over the years, and we asked the respondents to grade the answers on a scale of 1 to 5. Then we multiplied the factor of importance by the number of replies and added the totals together to get an aggregate. Here are the final results:

1.	Sermons	4072
2.	Friendliness	3201
3.	Music/Choir	2700
4.	Personal Friends Here	2653
5.	Sunday School Program	2475
6.	Body Life	2152
7.	Youth/College Career	2031
8.	Visit by Chapel Representative	1528

By far, once an individual walked into the Chapel, it was the pulpit ministry that caused them to remain. Of the 900 surveys, 752 rated "Sermons" as being "Very Important" in causing them to stay. The next highest was "Friendliness" with 335 votes.

We have repeated this same survey with every new members class since the original survey. This involved 80 to 100 people each year. The results have never varied as to the importance of the pulpit.

Those who preach and speak, even when not using the Word of God, but merely giving their own ideas and concepts, have always been instrumental in changing the course of history and people's personal lives. Lloyd-Jones comments,

> It is a very interesting thing to note that some of the greatest men of action that the world has ever known have also been great speakers and orators . . . the general history of the world surely demonstrates quite plainly that the men who truly made history have been men who could speak, who could deliver a message, and who could get people to act as the result of the effect they produced upon them.[13]

How much more, then, when that speaker has for his subject material the awesome, eternal Word of God!

----

[1]Ken Parker, "Seven Characteristics of a Growing Church," *Church Growth Handbook*. Pasadena, CA: Institute for American Church Growth, 1979, pp. 61-68.

[2]Robert Schuller, "Three Characteristics of a Successful Pastor," *Church Growth Handbook*, pp. 92-94.

[3]Charles Mylander, "How to Build High Morale in Your Church," *Church Growth Handbook*, pp. 85-91.

[4]Win Arn, "How to Find a Pastor. . ." *Church Growth Handbook*, p. 12.

[5]*Ibid.*, p. 12.

[6]*Ibid.*, p. 14.

[7]Donald A. McGavran, *Understanding Church Growth*. Grand Rapids, MI: Wm. B. Eerdmans Publishing Co., 1970, p. 119.

[8]Haddon Robinson. "Leadership Forum: Power, Preaching, and Priority," *Leadership* (Winter 1980), Vol. I, No. 1, p. 17.

[9]*Ibid.*, p. 18.

[10]Haddon Robinson, *Biblical Preaching*. Grand Rapids, MI: Baker Book House, 1980, p. 39.

[11]Bob Smith, *When All Else Fails*. Waco, TX: Word Books, 1974, p. 58.

[12]McGavran, p. 20.

[13]D. Martyn Lloyd-Jones, *Preaching and Preachers*. Grand Rapids, MI: Zondervan, 1971, p. 12.

CHAPTER 6

Characteristics of an Effective Pulpit

If the pulpit is instrumental in church growth, a logical question follows: What kind of pulpit is effective? The qualities that I list here are based on a survey we took and my own personal experience over the years.

The survey was sent to about 120 individuals who had joined the Chapel in official church membership over the previous two years. It asked them five questions designed to determine the most valuable features of the pulpit ministry. The following eight factors are ranked according to the survey results.

1. Biblical
2. Instructive
3. Interesting
4. Illustrative

5. Logical
6. Warm
7. Positive
8. Humorous

The survey revealed that not only is the pulpit significant in church growth, but that a particular style of pulpit ministry is important.

What Kind of Preaching?

It Must Be Biblical Preaching

This is the most important point in the people's response to the pulpit. God has not promised to bless anything else or anything less than His Word. Our congregation at Jacksonville Chapel is 60% to 70% former Roman Catholic. Their constant testimony is that they have learned more Bible in six months here than they learned all the balance of their lives. Our emphasis on the Bible is a major attraction.

Effective pulpiteers have always realized that the Bible was a necessary emphasis. Clarence Macartney, one of the most effective Presbyterian preachers ever to occupy a pulpit, believed this to be the force behind the pulpit. Concerning the pulpit ministry he said, two days before he died, "Put all the Bible you can into it."[1]

Our preaching must be filled with the Bible. To offer anything else is to betray God and to deprive man. Those who have substituted something other than the revelation of God have not fully understood the need of man. Lloyd-Jones said it well:

> The moment you consider man's real need, and also the nature of the salvation announced and proclaimed in the Scriptures you are driven to the conclusion that the primary task of the Church is to preach and to proclaim this, to show man's real need and to show the only remedy, the only cure for it.[2]

It Must Be Expository Preaching

One cannot improve on "the mind of the Spirit." The most accurate way to carry the mind of the Spirit is through expository preaching. If the passage speaks of justification in a particular context, then I believe that the Spirit of God is showing how justification is interwoven in the warp and woof of that context. As Robinson says, "First and above all the thought of the Bible writer determines the substance of an expository sermon."[3] If I preach a Biblical truth, I should present it at the address where it lives.

The most significant and helpful book I've read in recent years is Haddon Robinson's volume, *Biblical Preaching*. I never had the advantage of such teaching at seminary, so the contents of the book were a challenge and somewhat of a revelation to me. Perhaps most helpful of all was his succinct definition of expository preaching:

> Expository preaching is the communication of a biblical concept, derived from and transmitted through a historical, grammatical, and literary study of a passage in its context which the Holy Spirit first applies to the personality and experience of the preacher, then through him to his hearers.[4]

That says it all. The definition not only taught me, but as a good poem does, it expressed for me the thoughts and concepts that have boiled inside me for years. One major change I have made because of Robinson's book (and because of advanced courses taken at seminary) is that I have more carefully explored and used the concept of the "big idea" or the homiletical idea. I have tried to discipline myself of late to gather that one idea above all others.

It Must Be Incarnational Preaching

Robinson's definition said that the Holy Spirit first applied the truth "to the personality and experience of the preacher." Fundamental churches throughout the land, even in my own neighborhood, heartily ascribe to the above emphasis and the above definition. But some of them are dead, dull, and deteriorating. Their doctrine is orthodox, their separation is almost clinical, and yet the pulpit is anything but effective. I seriously suspect that for them, the Word has become a tool to be used rather than truth to be lived.

Lloyd-Jones warned, "So let us be clear that we are not to talk about the gospel as if it were something outside us. We are involved in it; we are not to look at it just as a subject to say things about; it itself is directly presented and conveyed to the congregation through us."[5] He says elsewhere, "the whole personality of the preacher must be involved . . . that it is 'truth mediated through personality'"[6] (quoting Philip Brooks' famous definition).

A man never really preaches a sermon, he preaches himself. I have watched the many young seminary graduates on our staff, and could quickly discover those who were enjoying their Christian life and those who were finding it a burden. This is why I've always asked them to preach simple messages so that they could convey more of themselves. Michael Tucker, pastor of the innovative Pulpit Rock Church in Colorado and an effective communicator, observed, "Part of the dynamic of preaching is that the preacher first deals with the passage as it touches his own life. Only after the Scripture has spoken to me can I speak with authority to others."[7] If the preacher is not enjoying his own walk with God, then the path he proclaims will seem to be dreary and uninviting. Again, to quote Robinson, "The audience does not hear a sermon, they hear a man."[8]

Herein lies the personal value of expository preaching. A man must grapple with the text. He must wrestle Heaven's reality and he is changed because he has "been touched on the thigh" to walk differently. Robinson recognizes the linkup when he says, "Regrettably, many preachers fail as Christians before they fail as preachers because they do not think biblically."[9]

It Must Be Positive Preaching

The early years of my Christian life burdened me with an awesome, gloomy concept of God. My preaching was often harsh and guilt-ridden. Unless I made an audience feel guilty and ashamed of their performance as Christians, I felt I had not done an adequate job.

A change began to take place in me, Scripturally and psychologically. I began to see that the Bible was not a "problem" book but an "answer" book. Life was not to be a drag but a delight. I began to reflect on the fact that Jesus Christ did not speak of His crucifixion unless He linked it immediately to His resurrection, something very positive. God talked about sin abounding only in the context of superabounding grace.

Over the years in my many seminars on Biblical self-image, I have always carried out a little experiment. Whether I am dealing with young people or missionary candidates, I ask the audience, "How many of you know Romans 3:23?" Usually, a score of hands are raised. The verse is overwhelmingly negative—"For all have sinned and come short of the glory of God." Then I ask, "How many know Romans 3:24?" I have never yet found an audience that has known that verse; and yet that negative in Romans 3:23 is inextricably linked up to the positive remedy of the free grace of God in Romans 3:24. God, it seems, always links negatives to positives.

The results of positive preaching soon become obvious. People begin to like God. A young Roman Catholic girl who began coming to the Chapel called me one morning after about a month's attendance to say that she had accepted Christ. I asked her what had developed her interest. She said that she had left her church when she was about 14 because she always felt that God was angry with her. Then she said, "The first time I attended the Chapel, I left saying to myself, 'I think God likes me.'" That's what it's all about.

Other evangelicals have realized that the negative is a major problem among fundamentalists. Tucker says,

> Most of us were either raised or exposed to a fundamentalism or evangelicalism that taught us to be negative. We emphasize man's sinfulness. We try to motivate ourselves and others through guilt. Have you ever noticed how much our evangelical preaching is negative? Even when we preach on joy our emphasis is, "You are not joyful enough." ... We try to get Christians in gear by making them feel guilty, but the New Testament does not do that.... The good news is that as Christians God is pleased with us.[10]

Francis Schaeffer said, "God meant Christianity to be fun."[11] Positive preaching sets the mood and gives people the impression that God indeed is to be enjoyed.

It Must Be Victorious Preaching

Two important qualities in good preaching are the admission of humanity by the preacher and the possession of a healthy self-image.

The Admission of Humanity. I am a firm believer that the preacher should admit his own failure. By this I don't mean a morbid self-disclosure, but a continual communication that he constantly needs God's grace for himself. By this he not only communicates honesty but reminds his hearers that God's grace is victorious. Paul speaks of his own despair in 2 Corinthians 1. He mentions Timothy's weakness. This kind of emphasis says to a congregation that even though we fail and sin, God's grace is victorious.

Should our audiences ever get the impression that we are anything but fellow pilgrims, struggling with the same problems as they do, they will not identify with us nor believe that our message is practical. The preacher communicates that God works with him too and, in spite of his shortcomings, failures, and sin, the grace of God is sufficient. Lloyd-Jones comments on the rapport the preacher is to have with the audience: "Surely preaching involves . . . a direct contact between the people and the preacher, and our interplay of personalities and minds and hearts."[12] I know of no better way to do that than to let people know we also get our feet dirty on the pilgrim journey.

The Possession of a Healthy Self-Image. If Christianity leaves us in the mire and the slough of despondency, then we ought to seek something else. Of course, it does not. Paul said, "I would to God, that . . . all who hear me this day, might become such as I am, except for these chains" (Acts 26:29). The Word should have permeated the preacher so that he understands, in spite of his failures and problems, his exalted position in the eyes of God.

The gospel has a pragmatic value—it works. Self-respect, dignity, and poise belong to him who truly understands the gospel. People do not like to listen to self-abnegation or self-deprecation. They are beaten down enough in the outside world without having to be exposed to it on Sunday. If the pastor is struggling and dissatisfied as an individual, he cannot hide it from the pulpit. His sermons are not so much lectures but demonstrations of his life. Robinson said in a forum discussion, "When a man preaches he reveals himself, and if he does not reveal himself, he has in fact revealed himself."[13] And when he does, the congregation understands whether he's enjoying his Christianity or not.

It Must Be "Warm" Preaching

The pastor must convey to his audience that he likes them, that he enjoys them, that he is glad they are there, and that he is glad he's a representative of God. Reverend Richard Cecil (quoted by Lloyd-Jones) sensed the difference when he said, "To love to preach is one thing, to love those to whom we preach is quite another."[14] This is hard to contrive, but difficult to do without. Lloyd-Jones sounds a warning.

The preacher must never be "clinical." So often the preacher is. Everything he does is right, is indeed almost perfect; but it is clinical, it is not living; it is cold, it is not moving, because the man has not been moved himself.[15]

Discussing the need for warmth, Lloyd-Jones said, "A theology which does not take fire, I maintain, is a defective theology; or at least the man's understanding of it is defective. Preaching is theology coming through a man who is on fire."[16]

A man gripped by what he is saying reveals the warmth of God. He loves as God loves, and his people feel the glow from the pulpit.

Often I make personal references to people in the audience. I use illustrations that involve them (with their permission, of course). We are friends, and they should know it. I often use humor or family illustrations to convey the fact that I am a warm human being. I avoid the use of the word "pastor" or "reverend." We are all on a first-name basis and I like it that way.

It Must Be Relevant Preaching

Preaching must be people-centered and "times"-centered. People must understand that Biblical truths work for their problems. Sangster talks about the discouragement that sometimes comes to modern preachers:

> Some men have half consciously lost faith in the message itself and its ability to meet the need of the world in any wide way. What relevance has evangelism, they ask, in an age that toys with atomic bombs . . . other men have grown weary of offering what so few seem to want.[17]

Discouragement will come if we fail to realize how much the gospel can deal with personal and timely problems. The most difficult part of our preparation, or sermonizing, is to make our messages meaningful to our audiences. Yet this difficulty should not stop us from achieving that goal. Lloyd-Jones pleaded, "It is always our business to be contemporary; our object is to deal with the living people who are in front of us and listening to us."[18] Robinson also pleaded, "A preacher, therefore should forget about speaking to the ages and speak to his day."[19]

A high degree of relevance can be attained in several ways:

Through current reading. The preacher should constantly peruse secular and Christian material. Once a congregation knows that you value good material, they will often give you articles they have discovered.

Through constant evangelism. Personal evangelism keeps us attuned to the man in the street. It is a valuable educational process.

Through counseling. Some of my best sermonic material has been created through accumulated years of counseling.

Through personal conversation. Even at social events, I am always probing people to discover where they are.

Through family experiences. Outside of Scriptures, I know of nothing as instructive as raising a family in helping me understand the problems of people.

It Must Be Exciting Preaching

I want to convey to my people the excitement of following Jesus Christ. Christianity is a growing process, always with new vistas and new challenges. Lloyd-Jones says, "A 'dull preacher' is a contradiction in terms; if he is dull he is not a preacher."[20]

Mike Cocoris, in his course on modern evangelism, made the point that a preacher must be an entertainer. He qualified that by saying that he did not mean a comic, but when a man stands before an audience of more than 100 people, he can no longer speak to them as a small, personal group. Excitement is wedded to the preacher's "stage presence." In his excitement, he should capture and hold an audience.

Many other characteristics help create and maintain an effective pulpit, but as Robinson defined expository preaching, "the Holy Spirit first applies [the Bible concept] to the personality and experience of the preacher, then through him to his hearers."[4]

The Methodology of an Effective Pulpit

Preparation

Enough cannot be said about effective preparation. One is always preparing—counseling, life experience, and study, are all geared to effective preparation. No book I've ever read on preaching fails to stress that hard work is necessary. Robinson said of good preaching, "All its diamonds do not lie exposed on the surface to be picked like flowers. Its richness is mined only through hard intellectual and spiritual spadework."[21]

Lloyd-Jones adds,

> The preparation of sermons involves sweat and labor ... it is like a potter fashioning something out of clay or like a blacksmith making a shoe for a horse: you have to keep on putting the material into the fire and to the anvil and hit it again and again with a hammer. Each time it is a bit better, but not quite right; so you put it back again and again until you are satisfied with it or you can do no better.[22]

A pulpit calendar has been one of my most difficult problems. So many interruptions and changes of plan occur in a normal pulpit ministry that I have never been able to effectively put together a pulpit calendar. I cannot guarantee that the material that I have prepared will fit into the time slot that fluctuates depending on what is included in a morning service. This gets to be very frustrating at times.

Lloyd-Jones is opinionated about many things and he has some strong words to say about preaching calendars. He feels that it interferes with the freedom of the Spirit. "I have known men who, at the beginning of a season, after a vacation, would actually hand out a list of their texts for many months ahead and would indicate what was going to be preached every particular Sunday during that period of time. I reprobate that entirely and completely."[23]

I don't feel as strongly as Mr. Lloyd-Jones about it, but I've never been successful at it, though it does seem to have merit. I do, however, plan for several months ahead.

Basic exegesis. Especially in the New Testament, where Greek remains fairly familiar, good exegesis is the groundwork of the sermon. The Old Testament still presents some problems for the exegete who has not kept up with his Hebrew. It is during this time of exegesis that the exegetical idea should be stated and the homiletical idea formed. Lloyd-Jones stressed the importance of arriving at a single focus when he said,

> I cannot overemphasize the importance of arriving at the main thrust, the main message of our text. Let it lead you, let it teach you. Listen to

it. Then question it as to its meaning, and let that be the burden of your sermon.[24]

An outline. The outline should express in logical progression the flow of the message. At this point the verbal illustrations should begin to take shape and any visual aids should start to surface.

The manuscript. Every message should be written out. This practice establishes transitions, forces correct grammar, and allows for the creativity of literary phrasing. It also clarifies your thoughts and develops new thoughts. The manuscript should be typed so that you can have a clear text from which to study.

The visuals. Once the message has been written down, you should search for ways in which visuals might help convey the message.

Congregational outline. This is given to the congregation on Sunday morning to enable them to follow the message. It may contain fill-ins and other devices. It is more concise and educational than the homiletical outline.

The pulpit outline. A small outline should be taken into the pulpit and used for the purpose of placing the visuals in sequential order. The manuscript must never be taken into the pulpit. If possible, the outline should never be referred to. One should always preach without notes.

Memorization. Lloyd-Jones felt that memorization is restrictive. "To memorize this written sermon, is to me almost as bad . . . my chief reason is that it binds the man, it interferes with the element of freedom."[25]

I believe just the opposite. Memorizing the major part of the material gives the preacher a solid base to return to and thereby grants him more freedom. Some complain that memorization is hard work, but after you've spent hours studying and writing, most of the message is already part of your system. The benefits of memorization outweigh the cost. Also, it becomes easier over the years.

Practice. I always make it a point to preach the message at least once and sometimes twice in an empty room before I ever stand in the pulpit. When I do this, I integrate the visuals just as I would do during a service.

Robinson advocates practicing. He says,

Along this line of preparation, one of the best communicators I know, although he's been preaching for 25 years, goes into the empty sanctuary on Saturday night and preaches his sermon through twice to the empty pews so that he can stand up Sunday morning without a note. He has built a strong pulpit ministry because of this kind of rigorous discipline in preaching.[26]

I practice early Sunday morning before the first service. This enables me to enter the pulpit with confidence and enjoy and participate in the service. I think there is nothing more annoying than to see a pastor going over his notes while the rest of the congregation sings and worships.

Prayer. I always allow myself at least 15 minutes before I leave my study to have a personal time of prayer. In addition to this, I meet with my staff and others immediately before the services begin to engage in prayer.

Presentation

Audience warm-up. This sounds crass, but I mean simply putting the people in a receptive frame of mind. This is done by good, hearty singing, humor, some audience banter and excellent upbeat music. All of these prepare the soul to enjoy and worship God.

Animation. I am committed to good physical movement. If it were not for the overhead projector, I would do away with the pulpit entirely. This, of course, necessitates a lapel or a cordless microphone that enables the preacher to walk around.

Absolutely no notes! The greater the degree of dependence upon notes, the less creative the communication.

Evaluation

Always seek feedback from those whom you trust and respect.
Seek formal feedback periodically through some type of survey.
Listen constantly to yourself on tapes.
View yourself on TV monitors if possible.
Allow the message to be examined and scrutinized in small group sessions. This has a startling effect upon a preacher. Sometimes it is rather shocking to discover how little is retained and how much is misunderstood, especially after several days. Each Sunday, I submit to the congregation an outline with a questionnaire dealing with sermon application. They use the outlines when

they discuss the sermon in "Body Life" sessions on Wednesday evening. This is an objective appraisal of what you have really communicated. For a sample outline, see Appendix A.

I believe I am engaged in the greatest and holiest work of all—the proclamation of the Word of God. Any growth without that emphasis at its core creates a suspicion in me. It is an engaging and glorious task that has been neglected by studies on church growth.

---

[1]Clarence E. Macartney, *The Making of a Minister.* p. 18.

[2]D. Martyn Lloyd-Jones, *Preaching and Preachers.* Grand Rapids, MI: Zondervan, p. 26.

[3]Haddon W. Robinson, *Biblical Preaching.* Grand Rapids, MI: Baker Book House, 1980, p. 20.

[4]*Ibid.*

[5]Lloyd-Jones, p. 68.

[6]*Ibid.,* pp. 81, 82.

[7]Michael Tucker, *The Church: Change or Decay.* Wheaton, IL: Tyndale, 1978, p. 173.

[8]Robinson, *Biblical Preaching,* p. 24.

[9]*Ibid.,* p. 25.

[10]Tucker, p. 173.

[11]Francis A. Schaeffer, *True Spirituality.* Wheaton, IL: Tyndale, 1972, p. 164.

[12]Lloyd-Jones, p. 227.

[13]Haddon W. Robinson, "Leadership Forum: Power, Preaching, and Priority" *Leadership* (Winter 1980) Vol. I, No. 1, p. 20.

[14]Lloyd-Jones, p. 92.

[15]*Ibid.,* p. 89.

[16]*Ibid.,* p. 97.

[17]W. E. Sangster, *The Craft of a Sermon.* Philadelphia: Westminster Press, 1951, p. 22.

[18]Lloyd-Jones, p. 138.

[19]Robinson, *Biblical Preaching.* p. 27.

[20]Lloyd-Jones, p. 87.

[21]Robinson, *Biblical Preaching,* p. 21.

[22]Lloyd-Jones, p. 80.

[23]*Ibid.,* p. 189.

[24]*Ibid.,* p. 204.

[25]*Ibid.,* p. 228.

[26]Robinson, *Leadership,* p. 19.

CHAPTER 7

Organization—
Friend, Foe,
or Folly?

Every age knows the temptation to forget that the Gospel is ever new. We try to contain the new wine of the Gospel in old wineskins—outmoded traditions, obsolete philosophies, creaky institutions, old habits. But with time the old wineskins begin to bind the Gospel. Then they must burst, and the power of the Gospel pours forth once more. Many times this has happened in the history of the church. Human nature wants to conserve, but the divine nature is to renew. It seems almost a law that things initially created to aid the Gospel eventually become obstacles—old wineskins. Then God has to destroy or abandon them so that the Gospel wine can renew man's world once again.[1]

Those words were written by Howard Snyder. They reflect my own feelings as I've struggled with the creation of new organizational systems to meet Scriptural patterns and cultural needs.

The Organizational Dilemma

Many pastors lament that they have inherited an organizational structure that has taken on the aura of Moses' tablets. Any attempt to alter it is seen as encroaching liberalism or an iconoclastic disregard of "the way it's supposed to be." Structures tend to become an end in themselves and a hindrance to the expression of New Testament vitality. Trueblood saw this years ago.

> It is possible for the church to exist with a show of success, and still fail in its essential function. It is always failing when it becomes an institution which is bent on saving itself. It cannot save the world if it demonstrates an obsession with material things.[2]

Entrenched organization can not only stifle New Testament witness, but can cause more frustration among pastors than any other single factor in the life of the church. Most will admit that they spend an inordinate amount of time in administration, a testimony not to good organization but to the lack of it. John Alexander laments the difficulty.

> How many thousands of man-hours have been wasted at board meetings—meetings of Trustees, Directors, Elders, Deacons, Superintendents, Teachers or any Advisory Board—because nobody had a clear enough concept of what the board was supposed to do and what the individual board members were supposed to be doing?[3]

Organizational structure that is time-consuming and ineffective is not good organization. But we should not reject a concept merely because it has been used ignorantly or we have had some negative experiences. If we assume that organization should reflect the body of Christ and its ministry, then form and structure take on exciting possibilities. They can further the work and ministry of Jesus Christ. Howard Snyder pleads for this approach.

> A church which intends to grow and serve the kingdom of God must be structured in harmony with the biblical understanding of the church. This is not to say that a church structured otherwise will not grow, for churches with the most diverse structures have obviously grown and survived. But a church not structured in harmony with biblical principles will never achieve the quality of growth and the authenticity of discipleship which God intends.[4]

He adds later that organizational structure facilitates the church's expression of itself:

> Quite simply, the criterion of biblical validity means that all church structures should in fact help the church be the church and carry out its mission. They should be structures which promote community, build disciples and sustain witness. Structures which in fact do this are valid; structures which do not are invalid, regardless of how esthetic, efficient or venerated they may be.[5]

The idea of organizational structure itself is valid, even though evangelicals are often reluctant to embrace anything that would appear to restrict spontaneity in ministry.

Should We Organize?

Some Christians, because they've had teaching on the ministry of the Holy Spirit, have erroneously assumed that organizational structures may stifle the ministry of the Spirit. It is difficult for them to believe that the Holy Spirit can operate through an organization. They would rather believe that He bypasses such puny human efforts and supernaturally does His work. John Alexander, who heads up the work with InterVarsity Christian Fellowship, has faced this kind of opposition. He writes,

> Let's face it; a large number of committed Christians are very suspicious of structure and are opposed to organization — to management of a group. A sure way for a speaker to receive nods of approval from a Christian audience is to make derogatory comments about organization, structure and authority. If you are a leader who believes in structure, brace yourself to receive criticism as a carnal stifler of freedom, creativity and the Holy Spirit.[6]

Anyone who has attempted to change an organization or create a new one, or who even insists that one should be followed, knows the sting of the kind of criticism that Alexander mentions. Michael Tucker also mentions this attitude. "Most church leaders see management as the enemy of ministry. They need to understand that proper management is ministry and that any effective ministry must have management to sustain and perpetuate it."[7]

One recent opponent of administration and organization in the local church is Larry Richards in his book, *A Theology of Church Leadership.* He claims that any attempt to organize the body of Christ is to fail to recognize that such organization already exists. He goes as far as to claim that such organization denies the headship of Christ and the freedom that should exist within the body. He believes that we are afraid to allow Jesus Christ to have His way.

> We are all afraid of what might go wrong if we abandon control. In human organization this is a very valid fear. We cannot in any social organization composed of independent wills, simply turn people loose. And unless there is a supernatural dimension to the church of Jesus Christ, we cannot afford to "turn people loose" in our churches either. . . . to let leaders control others in the church, we place chains on Jesus. We are struggling to retain what He asks us to surrender—control. For it is Jesus who is Lord.[8]

There are several problems with that kind of approach. First, Richards assumes that organizational structure and the "supernatural dimension" of the church are mutually exclusive. I see no problem with using structure to express the "supernatural dimension." When Jesus fed the 5000, He made them sit down in groups of 50's and 100's. That certainly was not restrictive in any sense, but facilitated the ministry. We certainly are not "placing chains on Jesus." We are allowing Him legitimate channels through which He can express himself.

Richards' own history, and indeed his present ministry, are a testimony to the problems created by this approach. The church with whom he is associated has known constant decline. Recently that church sold all of its buildings and is now meeting in homes. At last report, the church continues to decline. This is not a good recommendation for his methodology.

Although I am sure that Richards and others have good theological motivation, I'm not so sure about the broad-based rejection of organizational principles. Alexander suspects such a rejection might be an excuse for something else.

> A more practical reason a person may shy away from planning is that sculpturing statements of objectives, goals and standards is hard work. It is much easier to settle for vague generalizations . . . then too, some

people are lazy. They are afraid to agree to a job description and to adopt goals and standards which will disrupt their easygoing lifestyle.[9]

Definition

Management is getting work done through others. Almost every writer on this subject subscribes to this definition in some way. Alexander expands on this by quoting Lawrence Appley of the President's Association. "Management is guiding human and physical resources in dynamic organizational units which attain their objectives to the satisfaction of those served and with a high degree of morale and sense of attainment on the part of those performing the service."[10] When management and organization are viewed in this manner, then "management is a ministry to and with people, not a manipulation of them."[11] Or to go back to what Tucker said, "Proper management is ministry."

Biblical Justification

Evidence of God's commitment to organization is overwhelming. To ignore it or to diminish it is to deny the nature of God and what He has revealed of himself in the Scriptures.

The Creation
Whatever interpretation one makes of Genesis 1:1-3, it is obvious that God introduced order where chaos reigned. The earth is described as "formless and void" (Genesis 1:2). Then, when the Spirit of God operates on that state, order is developed out of chaos. Since that time, order is replete in the creation. Whether one stares through a microscope or a telescope, his mind is confronted with order. Indeed, an organism is life organized in such a complex and effective manner that even the Biblical writers stand in awe and worship.

Teaching
Explicit teaching. The Corinthian church, among its many sins, was terribly disorderly and chaotic. In 1 Corinthians 14, Paul dealt

with a worship service that, because of the spontaneity of tongues and prophecy, was especially disturbing. Paul regulated the worship so that individuals would speak one at a time, not with a babble of confusion. He justified his statement, saying, "Let all things be done properly and in an orderly manner." Chaos, then, would seem to be unspiritual.

Alexander goes as far as to say, "The solution to frustration and chaos is to commit ourselves to Jesus Christ and then endeavor, under His lordship, to manage our work effectively. Either we manage our work or the work manages us."[12]

Implicit teaching. The gifts listed as existing in the body of Christ refer to its organization. In Romans 12 we discover "one who leads" *(proistemi)* listed among the gifts. The word means "to stand before" and is sometimes translated "to govern." If this is one of the spiritual gifts, then obviously God provided for leadership within His body.

When instructing the church on the selection of elders, Paul lists a qualification that again suggests organization. He says that an elder "must be one who manages his own household well . . . (but if a man does not know how to manage his own household, how will he take care of the church of God?)" (1 Timothy 3:4, 5). Here again is the same word, *proistemi,* but in this passage it is translated, "manage." This is implicit evidence that management qualities are important in the affairs of God. When Richards says, "ministry, not administration, is the calling of the spiritual leader,"[13] his statement does not line up with the qualification and the function of elders as listed in the New Testament.

In Ephesians 4 Paul describes the maturing church as "the whole body, being fitted and held together by that which every joint supplies, according to the proper working of each individual part" (Ephesians 4:16). Whatever else this verse teaches, it describes an intricate and well-functioning organism. The body of Christ is highly organized. Life organized becomes an organism.

Illustrations

The Scripture not only has implicit and explicit teachings, but also abounds with illustrations of organization and management.

Battle plans. When we examine the campaigns of Abraham against the kings or Gideon's battle with the Midianites, we are observing clever and sophisticated planning. Some of Joshua's battles also show an exemplary degree of organization.

Camping in the wilderness. When the Israelites camped, it was a sight to behold. With the tabernacle in the center, the Levites in the next immediate circle, and then the twelve tribes surrounding the tabernacle symmetrically arranged with three tribes on each of the sides, a distant observer would be impressed with the organization. The directions given for moving the tabernacle, with the various families of the priests, is also an example of a highly organized arrangement.

Moses and the elders. Many writers mention the great example of Jethro, who counseled Moses on the selection of leaders. As Moses tried to take too much responsibility upon himself, his father-in-law counseled him to appoint others to share the burden. It is one of the finest examples of the delegation of authority.

Nehemiah the wall-builder. The book of Nehemiah serves as an example of how to get a job done. It contains principles of delegation of authority and motivation that are part of good management and administration.

The selection and training of the twelve disciples. Jesus' method of preparing leaders by training an inner three and then the remaining nine shows a commitment to organization. The feeding of the five thousand also shows classic organizational principles.

The developing church. The disposition of the widows in Acts 6 shows that the early apostles were not averse to good organization. It is widely held that here the first deacons were appointed to meet the growing needs. The principle of priority is especially in evidence here. The apostles were reluctant "to neglect the word of God in order to serve tables" (Acts 6:1). That's simple, good management.

The missionary journeys. Paul's method of going to the cities that were the centers of the ancient world reveals that he understood something of the economy of effort.

The Early Church

The early church emerged with a basic organizational structure intact. There were elders, or bishops, shepherds of the flock. In addition, some churches had deacons and perhaps deaconesses assisting in the ministry of the body. There also seemed to be a wider association in the councils, as indicated by Acts 15. Since Scripture lays down directions for the selection of elders and deacons, it would seem obvious that at least the basic skeletal structure is intact for the local body. Whether or not the council is to be perpetuated is open to question.

Summary

Organization in a local assembly is not only valid but important in carrying out its ministry. Snyder's three basic principles of organization are gleaned from a survey of the Scriptures.

1) Church structure must be biblically valid. Church structure must be a reflection of the gift-oriented arrangement as listed in the New Testament.

2) Church structure must be culturally viable. It cannot openly violate the cultural forms in which it finds itself. This is one of my major complaints about Richards' approach to local church ministry. The American culture is used to a church building. It is comfortable with coming to a service on a Sunday morning. Especially here in the Northeast, where the Roman Catholic background is so evident, to ignore that background unnecessarily is to cause problems that could easily be avoided. One can take advantage of the culture of Christmas or Easter or the religious culture in which one finds oneself, as long as he does not violate Biblical principles.

3) Church structure must be flexible. Further discovery of Biblical teaching, cultural norms, or philosophy of ministry should have a corresponding change of structure. None of us has a corner on all of God's truth. The more we discover it, the more we have to reflect that knowledge in our organizational patterns.

If we expect to achieve the work of God, then just as with any other work, we must plan and organize. This is never to diminish the supernatural dimension. Even though our organization is of this world, the product is not.

Organization must not only reflect New Testament teachings on the body and its gifts, but also be required to accomplish the God-designed ministry. The next chapter explains our growing effort to do just this.

[1]Taken from *The Problem of Wineskins* by Howard A. Snyder, pp. 15, 16. ©1975 by InterVarsity Christian Fellowship of the USA and used by permission of InterVarsity Press, P.O. Box 1400, Downers Grove, IL 60515.

[2]Elton Trueblood, *The Incendiary Fellowship*. New York: Harper and Row, 1967, p. 28.

[3]John Alexander, *Managing Our Work*. Downers Grove, IL: InterVarsity Press, 1975 p. 43.

[4]Taken from *The Community of the King* by Howard A. Snyder, p. 23. ©1977 by InterVarsity Christian Fellowship of the USA and used by permission of InterVarsity Press, P.O. Box 1400, Downers Grove, IL 60515.

[5]*Ibid.*, p. 97.

[6]Alexander, pp. 10, 11.

[7]Michael Tucker, *The Church: Change or Decay*. Wheaton, IL: Tyndale, 1978, p. 107.

[8]Taken from A THEOLOGY OF CHURCH LEADERSHIP by Lawrence O. Richards, pp. 200, 201. Copyright ©1980 by The Zondervan Corporation. Used by permission.

[9]Alexander, p. 20.

[10]*Ibid.*, p. 13.

[11]*Ibid.*

[12]*Ibid.*, p. 8.

[13]Richards, p. 80.

CHAPTER 8

Body Life

Gene and Lauren are relatively new at the Chapel. Here are Gene's encouraging words about our Body Life ministry:

> Not long after I accepted the Lord as my Savior at Jacksonville Chapel, I heard you mention something about "Body Life" from the pulpit one Sunday. To be quite honest with you, I thought it was some kind of Christian exercise class or something. A few days later someone called me and invited me to a Body Life meeting, and with some anxiety I accepted. I don't think I will ever forget that evening. Little did I know that I was about to meet the people who would become my closest, most loving friends.
>
> They welcomed this stranger into their midst and shared their love and fellowship with me. They prayed for my needs and reached out their hands unselfishly when we needed help. But most of all, they demonstrated to me what Christians were supposed to be like. They were filled to the brim with the love and joy of Jesus Christ.

Lauren and I have talked about Body Life many, many times and we
both agree that we would have a much narrower view of Christianity if
it were not for our participation in Body Life.... Body Life creates a
small church atmosphere within a large and growing congregation like
that of Jacksonville Chapel.

The term, "Body Life," as popularized by Ray Stedman, reflected
the recognition that each believer was supernaturally endowed
with the spiritual ability (gift) to affect growth and change in other
believers. Believing this to be an important but neglected ministry,
Stedman's Peninsula Bible Church changed the structure of their
evening service. It became an open, sharing service in which the
congregation of 600 to 800 people publicly voiced and responded to
specific needs and problems. The needs could be financial, material, psychological, or spiritual. Sometimes the needs were met
immediately that night; at other times arrangements were made for
giving long-term assistance. All of this is described in Stedman's
book, *Body Life* (Regal Books, 1972). His insights helped us con-
ceive and launch our own ministry, though we opted for a similar
format with smaller numbers.

Concept and Organization

I arrived at the Chapel in 1970, convinced that there was tremendous growth potential here. In two years we went to double services and then in 1973 we completed a 1000-seat auditorium. That
sufficed for a while and a few years ago we went to double services
again. Early in the ministry, we introduced the concept of the believer's responsibility for ministry and laid a foundation by preaching a series on the book of Ephesians. Soon after the completion of
that study, we started a Body Life movement that met in private
homes during the midweek.

We decided to focus upon a midweek rather than a Sunday service because we saw Sunday morning as a major time of celebration and instruction. However, this meant that we would bypass
the traditional Wednesday night prayer meeting.

Homes would be the scene of the meetings to provide a warm
atmosphere that would encourage intimacy. Snyder observed, "In

the midst of dignity and reverence, many a lonely believer inwardly cries out for the warm, healing touch of *koinoneia*. Believers need to know by experience that the most high God is also the most nigh God."[1]

The groups had to be small (10-20) in order to allow personal bonds to develop with trust and care. Large groups are not designed for this; they tend to intimidate people rather than encourage sharing. Anyone who has tried to run a testimony meeting in a Sunday night service has discovered this fact. Snyder once again remarks, "Whatever its value, the traditional church worship service is not well designed for intercommunication, for fellowship. . . . As Allen Watts commented caustically, 'Participants sit in rows looking at the back of each other's necks and are in communication only with the leader.'"[2]

The meeting had to allow for face-to-face confrontation.

The agenda would include Bible study, prayer, sharing, and a time of refreshment.

A leader would be appointed for each group and specially trained in group dynamics.

Though we did much preparation, we had not yet officially suggested a change. However, convinced of this refreshing approach, we decided to step out gingerly and put in place this new structure to facilitate ministering.

Though our theological concepts had been initiated by Ray Stedman's writings, we differed in one major area. According to his books, Peninsula Bible Church held their Body Life meetings on a Sunday night with some 800 people in attendance. We were not convinced that personal ministry could take place on that large a scale. Many, we believed, would feel intimidated by a large group and would not minister or be ministered to. We felt that not only the lack of intimacy but the opportunity for "grandstanding" and other problems would tend eventually to weaken the very Body Life concepts that were being promoted.

I understand now that Stedman has departed from some of his earlier practices because of these very things. Conversations I've had with members of Peninsula Bible Church have assured me that we have followed a more effective path. A quick review will help explain the theological and philosophical underpinnings of our Body Life ministry.

Scriptural Precepts

Paul's concept in Ephesians 4 was clear. These conclusions formed the basis of the principles we used.

The Process (Ephesians 4:11, 12)

The pastor-teacher equips the saints to mend, heal, or outfit for service. Saints get broken, bruised, and used in ministry. A teaching ministry exists not only to motivate apathetic or disinterested members, but to heal those warriors wounded in battle. Should this healing ministry not take place because the pastor-teacher is involved in other things (usually this is the case), the process would be largely aborted. As they were being equipped, the saints would do the work of the ministry and engage in the building up of the body of Christ. We call the building of the body *edification* and the work of the ministry *evangelism*, nomenclature perhaps not totally accurate but functional.

The Product (Ephesians 4:13-16)

The pastor-teacher equips the saints toward maturity. Some of the aspects of maturity are listed in this section. First, there is *unity*—the ability of believers to remain together despite the differences between them that always exist. Elsewhere Paul encouraged the believers "to maintain the unity of the spirit in the bond of peace" (Ephesians 4:3). We cannot create unity; we can only maintain or disrupt it. God created unity because we need each other.

A second aspect of maturity is *stability*. Paul says, "we should not be tossed about by waves and winds of doctrine, trickery, craftiness or deceitful schemers." Believers live in an antagonistic atmosphere. Stability consists in the ability to resist the adverse influences encountered so often by a believer. Paul says that we are to speak the truth in love in the midst of these kinds of circumstances. Stability means not only to survive but to succeed. It has both a negative and a positive side. We should not let ourselves be tossed and turned, but we should minister to the chaos.

Finally, maturity means *harmony* (Ephesians 4:16). We must recognize each other's different functions and the importance of each individual part. Paul's concept of the body of Christ is unity, not uniformity. Harmony is diverse people working together.

The Purpose (Ephesians 4:17-24)

Once we begin to produce mature people, it is possible for us to present an alternative lifestyle to the darkened world in which we live. In verses 17-24 the Christian who had enjoyed the process of being fitted for service now stood before the world a changed individual. He became an effective evangelizer.

But there had to be some change in the organization to permit, allow, and encourage such a dynamic to take place. Snyder criticizes the evangelistic efforts of the traditional churches, saying, "The books on New Testament methods of evangelism, for instance, are good, but they attempt to graft some New Testament methods into ecclesiastical structures which are decidedly not New Testament in nature."[3] Here then was the problem. We could not put new wine into old wineskins. Structures had to change.

The Body Life Ministry

We started four groups in strategic areas in our community. They met on Wednesday nights for Bible study, sharing, prayer, and fellowship.

The groups were not popular at first because people were not used to the openness that was necessary to make them work. They were still beset with the traditional mind-set that Christians were listeners, not participants. They were not sure that they could minister. Slowly, however, the months of preaching paid off. Some individuals began to see the concept work.

I remember well one night I shared in one of the groups a struggle that I was having in the ministry. Attending that evening was a CBS television executive who had been saved during one of our discussion groups. I can still recall the shock on his face at the end of my plea. He said, "Earl, I never knew you went through things like that. I thought you were above all that." That night he prayed for me in a way that I'd never been prayed for before. He and I both wept.

Awakenings like this one began to occur more frequently. People discovered the joy of ministry and the security of unconditional love.

Goals

Out of our beginning experience we set up some practical goals:
1. To grow personally in our walk with God.
2. To influence positively our family.
3. To have a positive attitude toward our job.
4. To be a channel of witness to unbelievers.
5. To be people full of good works in the community.

These were lofty goals, but wonderfully, we began to see a few of them realized.

Testimonies

Sig Volz. One young Chapel leader is a highly skilled machinist who has made a diligent and successful effort to develop a Christ-like home. In 1973 Sig went to his first Body Life meeting because he "wanted to do something." At that time he was shy and reluctant to speak, and for the first few months he said nothing. But he knew he was loved and accepted by the group, and slowly he began to participate. By the end of that first season he had matured so much that the leader asked him to be a co-leader the next year. The maturing process continued. He was eventually elected to the board and finally became an Assistant Zone Coordinator. He and his wife became so involved in the ministry that they actually built a beautiful new room on their home to use for the Lord. He had moved from the stands to the playing field to engage in God's wonderful game of ministry.

Jerry Allison, one of our Zone Coordinators, tells us more about him:

> I remember when Sig came to our Body Life group. First of all, I think he felt handicapped because he had come from Germany as a teenager, alone, and did not have mastery of the English language yet. One night, after Body Life, he said that he did not know where to start; that he was convinced he was gifted spiritually at the time of his conversion and that he could not get started. He was low on the list if you were picking leaders, and he could not get started anywhere in a ministry. He mentioned a couple of programmish possibilities that he had explored and volunteered for and nobody picked him up. I think that smarted a little bit. His expression was that he wanted to do it, and that's all I needed! There is a place for everybody that wants to do it.
>
> Sig was a giver from the word "go." He would give you anything

and even his home. He just says, "This is not my home. This belongs to the Lord. We want to make it available for people who want to serve Him."

Jim and Angie. Jim is a young attorney and Angie is his charming wife. They've had their share of difficulties with their young family, but from the following testimony we can see how the body of Christ ably ministered to them through their Body Life group:

> On August 5, 1985 Angie and I were blessed with Adam and Matthew, our twins. The new babies, along with Jimmy (5) and Louissa (3) almost destroyed us. In response, our Body Life group began supplying dinners every night for about two months. The meals themselves and, more importantly, the love behind those meals helped carry us through those difficult times. The dedication of these people was a true testimony to our family and friends who do not know the Lord.
>
> The twins, at two months of age, developed viral meningitis. Our group prayed us through this terrible time. Today the boys are fine with no residual effects from their sickness.
>
> Body Life has brought us closer to knowing Jesus Christ through the witnessing of the Holy Spirit at work in the saints of our group. Just as in any human endeavor, Body Life is not perfect. With the closeness comes disappointment, with caring comes hurt, but there is no doubt that Jesus Christ is reflected in the relationships allowed to develop at Body Life.

In my own Body Life group (we pastors rotate as much as possible but still enjoy going to our own local group) we were discussing the need for forgiveness of one another. One woman told us of a struggle she had been having. None of us was prepared for what she was about to reveal.

When she was a girl, her father, a city detective, would become very brutal at home. One night after a particularly violent argument he drew his pistol and began to threaten her and her mother. Both fled the apartment and ran down the stairs. He fired at the fleeing women and his first bullet struck and killed her mother. The second bullet struck this girl, but she managed to stay on her feet and run from the building, no mean feat for a 12-year-old girl. Her father was chasing her and firing. She recounted how the department covered up for her father and he was never imprisoned. Many years later, she said, he came to live with her.

When she was finished, we were all silent as we realized the kind of suffering this wonderful woman had endured. We also began to understand the triumph of the grace of God in her life. I shall never again talk to that woman without realizing the backdrop against which her life is played.

We discovered that Body Life bonded us to people in ways we could not anticipate. Paul speaks of "Weeping with those who weep." There is no greater bond than the tears of the saints.

Over the years stories like this have multiplied. Body Life people have cared for dying members, arranged car shuttles for those who had to have chemotherapy daily, taken over households that had known disaster, ministered to singles who have been rejected by other churches, and much, much more. The ministry achieved far more than we had imagined. We had tapped into a reservoir of spiritual care and giftedness that could never have been discovered or fulfilled by a traditional ministry.

Early Problems

As with any new ministry, early problems began to surface.

Groups tend to become ingrown so that newcomers sometimes feel unaccepted.

There are those in Body Life who are constant complainers, whose problems are aired but never solved. People grow tired of dominant, strident voices.

Since traditional Christians are used to going to meetings to *get* something, the common complaint about Body Life is that "I stopped going because I didn't get anything out of it." One wonders if they ever thought about giving something!

At times, some in the group may become overbearing and argumentative. I've led such groups and the dissatisfaction in the rest of the group is obvious. Sometimes a personal word after the meeting is necessary to make the offending member aware of what has happened. Sometimes you have to lose a member to save a group.

Leadership

At first we trained our four leaders every Sunday night an hour before the Sunday evening service. Since part of the Body Life meeting was Bible study, we provided a fresh study each week and reviewed it with the leaders so that they, in turn, could teach it at the group level. There would also be a time of discussion of problems that had arisen in their own Body Life groups. However, the major complaint of the leaders was that the material was so new to the groups that they spent an inordinate amount of time explaining, clarifying, and just getting exposed to the text. Body Life was actually being stifled trying to transmit information in the text. The leaders found themselves doing additional study even though we had supported them with a format.

We decided on a new approach. Since the entire congregation was together (leaders and participants) on Sunday morning, and since we engage in expository preaching, we decided to make the Sunday morning text the basis for discussion. This way, all would be exposed to the same study and there would be no "fresh" material each week. This meant, however, that it would be necessary to place in the hands of the people a simple outline that they could follow. We later added fill-ins to the outline as an educational tool. Since every modern congregation has a variety of Bible translations, we published a common text (usually the NASB), underneath the outline so that there would be a common point of reference. Now we had leaders and participants exposed to the same text and the same study, which they could review on Wednesday nights.

We were interested not just in people learning the Word but living it in practical situations. Therefore, we began to publish a series of questions called *Body Life Suggestions,* which dealt with the practical application of the text studied.

This proved to be a tremendous advancement over the former method. Leaders were not bogged down with extra study and the people were not coming "cold" to the session. Most would bring their outlines and Bibles with their notes and fill-ins completed.

Traditional Reluctance

Those who viewed the Wednesday night prayer meeting as possessing unusual sanctity resisted the Body Life ministry at first. Even though for years it was poorly attended, the prayer meeting was still considered the barometer of spirituality. Actually it was more an indicator of boredom and irrelevance. Rather than forcing the extinction of the prayer meeting, we allowed it to continue in addition to the Body Life meetings.

We also found that some people carried over into the Body Life meetings the mind-set cultivated by years of attendance at traditional Wednesday night prayer meetings. Some people still had the stereotype of a Christian meeting in mind—they were an audience, and the success of the meeting is judged by how the audience is amused or "blessed."

Philosophical Problems

Some people thought we were "forcing" Christian fellowship by our new structure. We were accused of creating molds that made people do things they were reluctant to do. But such really was not the case. We were eliminating structures that stifled Body Life. What people were really experiencing were birth pangs or transitional stretching.

It was amusing for a while to listen to the reaction of the Christian community. In our local Bible college some were circulating the rumor that we had gone liberal. Some were even questioning whether or not I was really saved.

One important aspect in any organization is its flexibility. Snyder comments, "Structures must be flexible. In those areas where no revealed pattern has been given, changes should be made as circumstances and Biblical fidelity warrant."[4] Problems simply become challenges that cause more effective organization to evolve.

Current Ministries

Because people began to take seriously their involvement in ministry, several remarkable new ministries evolved from Body Life. We did not anticipate all of them.

Counseling

Since it was now understood that "problems" were acceptable and did not detract from Christian standing, people began to mention things that had long been buried but never forgotten. At first the counseling load at the staff level began to increase, but then people began to realize that they not only were responsible for it but actually equipped to do it. We offered additional courses on counseling that became very popular. Couples within the Body Life groups became sensitive to others who had problems and would provide counsel and discipline when needed.

Prayer Partners

The groups averaged from 10 to 20 people. This was still a large number to provide a deeply personal approach, but people began to gravitate to others who showed interest or empathy. They sought prayer and fellowship outside the group itself.

Social Events

Each Body Life group became a close-knit unit. In fact, to this day when we have to divide groups because the numbers become too great, there is considerable resistance. The groups began to have their own socials. In the early years we had one huge Body Life meeting with all the groups involved in the middle of June. Since most of our ministries are canceled for the summer, we felt that this would be a good way to conclude the Body Life "season." It became the highlight of the year, at which individuals shared what the ministry had meant to them.

Missions

The Chapel long since recognized that proper personal attention was not given to many of our missionary families. The Body Life groups came up with the idea of each of them "adopting" their own missionary. In this way, they could minister through letters and special gifts even though the main financial support would still come from the main body of the Chapel. When the missionaries returned home they were hosted, cared for, and actually housed by the Body Life groups.

The Present Ministry

From that initial moment in 1973, Body Life has grown from four to 35 groups and is still expanding! Some 400 people are involved, and many more are touched who are not included in that number.

Other churches in the area heard about the success of Body Life, and we sent our staff to help other churches get started. But they seemed to face problems we had not encountered. Because the pulpit had not provided a strong Biblical background for the ministry, people were at a loss to understand the function of such groups, and many of them died. We also discovered that some pastors were threatened by groups that met without their presence. Many, rather than risk what they believed to be an "unguided missile," allowed them to die for lack of pastoral support.

Unless there is not only a constant Biblical affirmation of the ministry and a propounding flavor of acceptance from the pulpit, Body Life ministry has a difficult time surviving. The organizational structure must emerge from one's concept of the body of Christ.

We had moved from a "hallowed" Wednesday night prayer meeting in which 15 people met to listen to a Bible study and hear the same people pray long prayers divorced from personal needs, to a ministry that involves 400 people to care, share, and minister to one another. We not only increased personal growth potential and opportunities for ministry, but the entire prayer ministry as well.

Our first attempt at the distribution of the ministry to the people proved to be satisfying and successful. So glowing were the testimonies that constantly flowed from the Body Life ministry that we realized that we had made an excellent move. But we had only made a beginning.

---

¹Taken from *The Problem of Wineskins* by Howard A. Snyder, p. 97. ©1975 by InterVarsity Christian Fellowship of the USA and used by permission of InterVarsity Press, P.O. Box 1400, Downers Grove, IL 60515.

²*Ibid.*, p. 96.

³*Ibid.*, p. 23.

⁴*Ibid.*, pp. 124, 125.

CHAPTER 9

Zoning

Encouraged by our first serious attempt at restructuring for ministry, we were eager for even more. A study of the book of Joshua brought to light some of the principles of government used by the nation of Israel in its early days. These principles gave me the idea for "zoning."

1. Each tribe was responsible for the conquest and development of its own section of the land of Palestine.

2. Each section had its own priestly cities, teaching centers set aside for the priests, who would not have any claim on the land.

3. Cities of refuge were scattered throughout the land for easy access.

4. Even though each section was under the control and administration of one tribe, three times a year they all were to come to Jerusalem for a major celebration of worship.

Three Levels of Organization

Under this system there were three major units of ministry in the life of the people. First, there was the small unit, represented by the family or perhaps even the community. Then, there was the unit represented by the tribe and its elders who would hold the land in perpetuity. Finally, there was the large celebration represented by the three annual feasts.

With our new zoning concept, we were seeking to distribute the ministry of the Chapel along three similar lines. Years later in his book, *Secrets for Growing Churches*, Charles Mylander[1] discussed these three concepts at length. He used a threefold classification: *Celebration* (more than 200), *Congregation* (less than 200), and *Cell* (10-15).

I heartily agree with Mylander's classification, because at no time did I ever believe that the central pulpit ministry should be sacrificed on the altar of the small group ministry. With these three concepts in mind, the expository ministry would still continue to be formative and significant. Richards and Getz seemed to stress the small group concept so much that the pulpit was neglected. Our own experience had proved that, even though we had a ministry like Body Life, the key factor in the attraction and continued interest of people was the pulpit ministry.

I will use Mylander's nomenclature for this part of the chapter.

Celebration

I call it the "magic" of the Sunday morning service. Mylander describes it well.

> The church as celebration worships God with expectancy and joy. Any Christian can worship alone in the beauty of the woods or the majesty of the mountains, but the private experience of worship will never replace the public celebration of God's presence. Celebration radiates a festive mood and results only from a great gathering of like-minded worshipers. Faith and fervency change the atmosphere. The climate created by joyful singing, moving silence, or inspiring preaching contributes to the sense of the Spirit's presence. A spiritual celebration remains a personal matter, yet possibly only in concert with other people gathered for corporate worship.[2]

Snyder mentioned that the church needs periodic festivals.

I am not talking about superficial celebrations patterned after those of the world. Rather, I mean occasions which spring from and celebrate the genuine joy and excitement of corporately sharing the fact that God is active. This is what the Old Testament religious festivals were all about.[3]

He further adds, "The church must meet together regularly as a large congregation. It must actually come together as a people."[4] Here is where the flavor of the whole ministry is developed. Here is where the teaching that sustains all ministry goes forth. The Sunday morning service in its style, content, and impact reveals not only the magnificence of God but the whole philosophy of the congregation. By arranging the festivities of ancient Israel, God gave a psychological and spiritual boost to His people.

Congregation

The zoning concept would divide our congregation into geographical area. It would create smaller groups of people knit together by the ministering families within the parameters of this new organization. A zone would contain originally about 200 people and would be a *community-located* ministry.

Cell

Already in place and functioning well were the Body Life groups of 10 to 20 individuals. These, in a face-to-face situation, cared, prayed, and ministered to one another.

Initiating the New Structure

In order to fulfill what I believed to be viable Scripture examples, I made the following proposal:

1. The Chapel would be divided into seven geographical zones that would include the 80 different municipalities our people came from.
2. At the head of each zone would be a "Pastoral Family Unit." The unit would be an established family who had displayed spiritual maturity.
3. In addition to the Pastoral Family Unit, we would assign other

families to work with the Pastoral Family Unit within the zone to assist them in ministering. These families would help with ministries like Body Life, hospitality, and visitation units.

4. The Chapel staff would hold periodic meetings with the Pastoral Family Units to instruct them in administration and acquaint them with new approaches and new people in the area. We would also hold seminars to train other units in their ministry.

To launch our program of zoning we selected key families from each of our seven zones and invited them to an initial meeting one Saturday morning. The meeting was well-attended and the concept was well-received. Many of these people had already been active in Body Life groups.

We made a big mistake. We had prepared well for the meeting and even handed out job descriptions for each of the different units. When those who were being considered for the Pastoral Family Units read what their job entailed, they almost went into a dead faint. We had tried to gather all that the ministry would entail on one sheet of paper, and it was overwhelming. We did not discover this until we followed up with personal calls. We were dismayed that literally no one would take the job of Pastoral Family Unit.

We fell back and regrouped discarding the job descriptions and softened the responsibility. We offered staff assistance. We changed the name from Pastoral Family Unit to Zone Coordinator (for a job description, see Appendix C). Further meetings showed that we would have to adjust our original dream until the concept and the people grew.

This all began back in 1976. We assigned a staff member to guide this ministry because we felt it was so important.

Present Status

The zoning concept is now the backbone of the ministry at Jacksonville Chapel. The Body Life ministry falls under the Zone Coordinators' direction. When I came to the Chapel there were 250 to 300 people in attendance; now each *zone* contains nearly this many people. Most of our board members came up through these ranks. People are observed in the Body Life ministry and in zone activities to see how they handle conflict and responsibility. This is a natural training ground for leadership.

Each zone now contains from three to five Body Life groups. The Zone Coordinators are responsible for their supervision. When a zone feels that it has a need for an additional Body Life group, it is responsible for starting it and maintaining it with training and supervision given by the pastoral staff. Each zone, however, includes many other ministries. The zones grew to become highly sophisticated and organized in their ministries.

The Church Board

For a while we limped along with a traditional board of trustees. In our inherited structure they were actually a board of elders and were a considerable advancement over that which I had known for twelve years in a Baptist church. In the Baptist church we had not only a democracy but a two-board structure. I had learned how much better it was to have a "republic" rather than a democracy, in a church governed by one board. Ken Kilinski remarks, "Having two boards is the equivalent of having two company presidents. The church must have one central governing board."[5]

A young IBM executive who had been active in Body Life and in the ministry of zoning was elected to the board. He came with a recommendation that the board be reorganized along newly developing ministry concepts. We should be structured around the different areas of ministry that had become a major part of the Chapel's life, he said. We should form subcommittees around the ministry gift clusters that could oversee what was happening. The board, after studying his suggestions, adopted a new structure. Unless new developments necessitated a change, the structure would now be something like this:

The board would be grouped around basic "gift clusters":

Care —compassion, assisting those in need, hospitality.
Administration —organization, programs, personnel.
Missions —world evangelism, missionary correspondence.
Education —instruction, information and discipling.
Outreach —local evangelism, visitation, witnessing.

All activities in the Chapel would be classified under one of these committees. Besides the five CAMEO groups, there were two others: **W** for Worship and **Y** for Youth. These last two group functions, however, would take place centrally in the Chapel rather than being administered throughout the zones (see Appendix B).

Each committee would contain at least one board member and one member of the pastoral staff. Kilinski noted the wisdom of this arrangement when he said,

> The best way to provide this unity is to have each committee chaired by a member of the official board. Thus the board is not only a policy making body, but it also links together all the activities of the church. This arrangement allows board members to keep their fingers on the pulsebeat of the work of the church; simultaneously, it allows the workers who have problems or ideas to get them quickly to the board without being lost or garbled by a long chain of communication.[6]

Each committee could select those in the congregation they thought were particularly gifted in their ministry areas. These people could include nonmembers. All other ministries would report to these committees (see Figure 1).

At each board meeting the committee chairmen would report in writing, summarizing the activities of the past month and giving suggestions for necessary action. There would be a copy of each report for each board member. (A recent change has been made — board reports must now be ready the Sunday before the meeting so that members can peruse them beforehand.)

Here was a further attempt at the distribution of the ministry, but within accountable guidelines. We now have one major board meeting a month that lasts approximately 2½ hours. These twelve men, along with the pastoral staff, shepherd a church of 1800 to 2000 people. More and more the board members are being chosen from those who have revealed leadership qualities within the zones. Here again, organization not only facilitated ministry but provided for it, as leadership naturally emerged.

The board was now grouped according to CAMEO. Each ministry of the Chapel was included under one of the major headings. Our pastoral staff was also aligned according to the same acrostic. We had a full-time staff person in charge of Care, Administration, Missions, Education, and Outreach. Each letter of the acrostic

Pastoral Staff and Trustee Board
Pastor-Committee Ministries

Care • Administration • Missions • Education • Outreach

	C COMMITTEE	A COMMITTEE	M COMMITTEE	E COMMITTEE	O COMMITTEE
ZONE 1					
ZONE 2					
ZONE 3					
ZONE 4					
ZONE 5					
ZONE 6					
ZONE 7					

Figure 1. Full Spectrum Ministry

represented a committee headed by at least one board member and corresponding pastor.

Now we would need a way to unify the central board, pastor, and the ministering zones to ensure appropriate distribution of ministry resources and opportunities, development and achievement of sound goals, constant awareness, and informed prayer support throughout.

The Board-Zone Interface

Several tensions began to surface. With the increasing emphasis on the zoning concept and its place in our ministry, some wondered whether the board was sensitive enough to the needs of our zones. Were the ideas and suggestions that frequently surfaced in the zones affecting the direction the board was taking on certain issues? We soon felt we had two separate entities on our hands. Although one committee on the board, the Care Committee, had a major part in responding to the zone ministries, many felt that it was not enough.

In 1970 we had 250 to 300 people and a twelve-man board to govern and guide that group. Now, each *zone* had at least that many or more! How could one original board oversee that many people? Were we not depriving the zones of proper administration and counseling? Most Zone Coordinators were experiencing overload and burnout.

Besides this, the needs of the new ministries were not being communicated to the congregation adequately. Announcements in the bulletin seemed like the best way to relegate the ministry to obscurity! Even verbal pulpit confirmation was not enough.

I liked Alexander's observation:

> It is my personal conviction that a major cause for frustration in Christian organization is the morass of ambiguity: dedicated workers who yearn to serve the Lord are bogged down by uncertainty about what they are supposed to be doing, what is expected of them and how they can perform the work most effectively. Such confusion is a sad commentary on the leadership of such groups where scarcely anything is done in terms of goals and standards.[7]

Since we were committed to seeing each zone as almost a church within itself, we felt that it might be best to equip each zone with its own "board."

One man in the congregation, an extremely gifted, talented individual, realized our problems and spent weeks working with a new concept, a Board-Zone Interface.

The new structure, first of all, provided the Zone Coordinator with a team of people who served as a miniature board within the zone to facilitate the ministry in that area. Just as every pastor needs a team of leaders to help with the ministry, each Zone Coordinator needed an identical team for his geographical area. This team would be modeled after the classification headings already existing on the board, that is, CAMEO. For example, Zone 1 would have a Zone Coordinator who would be assisted by couples or individuals who would be in charge of Care, Administration, Missions, etc. We called this a "full-spectrum" ministry (see Figure 2). This alignment we affectionately called ZIP (Zone Input Panel).

A second structure would maintain a vital link between the board and pastoral staff and the ministering zones. Without that link the zones were liable to be isolated in a ministry all by them-

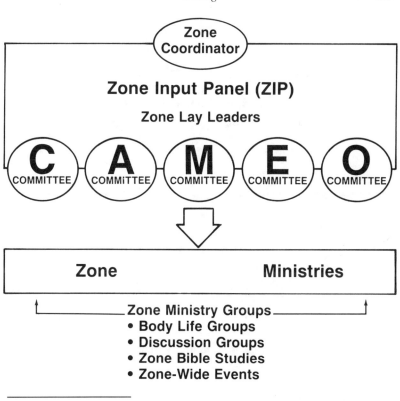

Figure 2. Zone Input Panel

selves and left without a voice in the major church-ruling body. We felt they would also be cut off from the pastoral training and policy changes in the main Chapel thrust.

In addition to the board setup we had the seven zones, each with its corresponding CAMEO structure. All totaled here were seven C's, seven A's, seven M's, etc. We decided that when the Care Committee met, the seven Care people should meet with the committee and pastor in charge of Care. This would help the committee understand what the special problems were in the zones and give additional insight. This would increase communication from the board to the zones as to its major goals, policy changes, and programs. The board, then, would be constantly aware of the needs within the zones, and the zones would now be aware of the

Figure 3. Zone Awareness Panel

board's direction and philosophy. This would help eliminate a problem Alexander emphasized. "When disgruntlement starts to fester within an organization, poor communication is invariably one—if not the major—explanation."[8]

A second important benefit was to allow the Care Pastor, Outreach Pastor, etc. to give his people personal training and input. Now each Zone Coordinator would have the confidence that his people were getting adequate training and direction.

This structure was known as ZAP (Zone Awareness Panel; see Figure 3). The Chapel, because of this new communication and guidance, could now mobilize more quickly and more effectively for all pan-church activities. Bulletin announcements became almost superfluous. The structure helped facilitate and guide the ministry.

Procedures and Problems

At first it seemed a horrendous undertaking, but we felt we had to do this or eventually lose the whole zone ministry. We prepared a series of steps to take and a suggested timetable for putting the structure in place. Here are some of the steps:

1. The staff reviewed a master list of all the people in the Chapel zones. We placed beside their names one or two of the letters in CAMEO that described their gifts. The same list was reviewed by the Zone Coordinators, and they also inserted their letter designations.

2. The final list was reviewed by the board for censure. If any board member censured a name, then that selection became doubtful, but that did not automatically disqualify the person.

3. The resultant list was then revised by the Pastoral Care Committee.

4. The final list of suggested names was then forwarded to the Zone Coordinators, who made the final choice. By this time he would have only six names on hand.

5. Because there were seven zones and six individuals needing to be named from each zone, we had to come up with a list of approximately 45 people, including alternates.

6. People eagerly responded. The minister of Pastoral Care organized simple training techniques and explanations. This structure has been in place now for three years, and already it has proven exemplary. Feedback from the pastors and the zones has shown this to be the desperately needed solution. For a synthesized view of the ZIP-ZAP structure, see Figure 4.

Now, in addition to the zones, we had in place an excellent structure for outreach and growth.

Problems

I would be less than realistic if I did not discuss some of the problems we continually face with our structured ministry.

People who do not fully grasp the philosophy behind the ministry, either because they are from a traditional ministry or new to the Chapel, complain about being overorganized. Since we take all complaints seriously, we constantly reexamine what we are doing

Living Stones

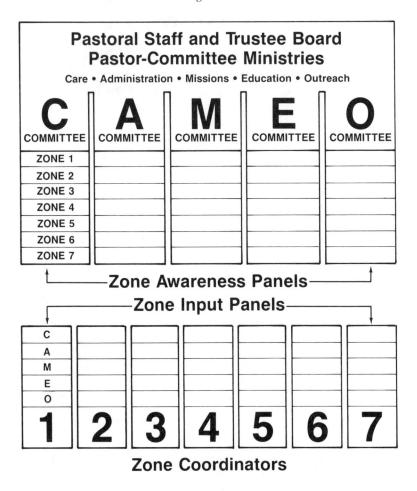

Figure 4. Complete Zone-Board Interface

to see if there is a simpler or better way. We have yet to discover one.

Because our coordinators have such responsibility, we constantly face the problem of burnout and overload. We have instituted Coordinator Meetings four times a year where we can inspire and motivate, but at the same time listen to their gripes and problems. One of our coordinators recently did a study of himself and his

CAMEO team to discover that they were all spending 50 to 60 hours a week in their secular jobs before they even began to carve out time for their families and for their ministries. We felt there should be a strengthening of the organization to delegate responsibility.

Since we add new staff from time to time, it takes a while to get them "up to speed" on the Chapel's philosophy and approach. This sometimes weakens their area of particular responsibility. Also, since our pastors have many other responsibilities, they tend at times to ignore their zone and strata responsibilities. (Strata are other groups organized according to specific ministry needs. They will be described in the next chapter.)

We also have a rotating board system so that four new board members (in a total of 12) are elected each year. They too take some time to get up to speed, and we have discovered that periodically we have to "reinvent the wheel."

As Senior Pastor, I can never assume that the congregation, since it is constantly changing and growing, is well-versed in zone and strata ministries. There must be a continued effort to reinforce the principles that have become so much a part of us. Even members who were once well-acquainted with the approach lose their perspective by attrition and so must be reminded over and over again of the Biblical approach.

But nothing is an unbridled success. Problems are merely challenges to fine tune our ministry. They don't discourage us from our main approach, no more than an argument should destroy a marriage. What we have tried and observed works—we found this out because our new structure would soon be severely tested.

The "Flood"

On April 5, 1983, our area was struck with its worst flood in 100 years. A second flood, though not nearly as serious, hit in May, a setback for many struggling to recover from the first flood. Three of our seven zones suffered badly. When the water receded, we realized that our philosophy of ministry and the structure we had put in place had been severely tested and had passed with flying colors. Our zones with their coordinators had been functioning for several years, so that an organization was well in place when the tragedy arrived. Our approach was as follows:

The first Sunday following the flood, after meeting with some Zone Coordinators, the Care Committee and some flood victims, we recorded both needs and resources and organized them to match resources with needs. A regular Sunday service was used to give people an opportunity to volunteer.

We organized the central Chapel to provide five major services: a flood office, food supply, clothing supply, baby-sitting, and a laundry service. To support these functions, we opened the kitchen and provided lunches for the volunteers. We maintained this high level of activity for two weeks, then reduced the effort the third week, keeping open the flood office and food and clothing supplies for limited hours.

A key ingredient in the effort was linking up resources in zones with needy zones; Zone 2 with 3; 4 with 5; 1 with 7; 2 and 4 with 6.

When the central phoning became jammed, we opened 14 other centers in the zones (two per zone) as information clearing centers. In addition, two resource zones conducted meetings to recruit help for needy zones.

We recruited "foreman" families to work with the flood victim families from the Chapel and tried to record progress from the central office for each victim family.

Additional attention was given to a number of non-Chapel people for cleanup, encouragement, and nontechnical counseling.

A great many other flood victim families used our food and clothing centers and our flood office provided additional help for others. A special benevolence offering was taken on the second Sunday following the flood, and a special committee established to disburse these funds. Our final disbursement was made in October that same year.

Statistical Summary

The Outreach ministry under Pastor Tom Clark's direction visited almost all 200 non-Chapel folk with an outreach packet.

The need was so massive, we prioritized our financial resources to help Chapel folk fully recover, then used remaining resources for others until the funds were depleted. Each case was judged in coordination with other sources of help to stretch our dollars as far as possible.

As of December, help was continuing for some in the form of labor, gifts and money.

Chapel units (family/single) who signed up to help:	374
Estimated number of other units who helped:	50
Total:	424
Estimated number of *individuals* involved in helping:	800

Kinds of help:

Cleanup	Skilled Labor	Clothing
Materials	Food, Meals	Financial Aid
Appliances	Counseling	Transportation
Information Centers	Laundry Service	
Pickup and Delivery	Baby-sitting	
Household contents	"Foreman Families"	

Victims/Household Units we helped:

Zone	Chapel-Related Folk	Non-Chapel-Related Folk	Total
1	0	1	1
2	1	1	2
3	19	44	63
5	41	116	157
6	17	35	52
7	7	3	10
	85	200	315

Financially assisted of the above:

	25 ($28,000)	25 (9,000)	50 (37,000)
Those not formally recorded (estimate)		25	

Though this report consists mainly of "sterile" facts, the real report is the story of people, trained and organized to minister, who left a remarkable impact upon the community. There were special teams of men who came to the stricken homes with sump pumps. An electrical team visited houses to ensure that no electrical fires would start. Special cleanup teams moved into homes that had been deluged with filthy water contaminated by local sewers. To assist these various teams, groups of women put together special cleanup packets, including disposable gloves for the workers. When a team invaded a home, another group of women prepared hot lunches and arrived on the scene to supply the day's meal. After the cleanup was accomplished it was sometimes discovered that whole walls had to be torn down because of wet insulation. The downstairs of many homes had to be rebuilt.

The major thrust of our ministry was handled by our Zone Coordinators and headed up by our Care Committee Chairman. Our minister of Pastoral Care provided the guidance and counsel necessary, but these men and their families (the Coordinators and CAMEO teams) pulled off a gargantuan effort that proved to us, once and for all, that we really have organized to facilitate and express ministry. We will never forget it.

This event validated our developing concepts, but our structure had been put in place not only for care but also for outreach and other ministries.

---

[1]Excerpts from SECRETS FOR GROWING CHURCHES by Charles Mylander. Copyright ©1979 by Charles E. Mylander. Reprinted by permission of Harper & Row, Publishers, Inc. p. 84.

[2]*Ibid.*, p. 85.

[3]Taken from *The Problem of Wineskins* by Howard A. Snyder, pp. 108, 109. ©1975 by InterVarsity Christian Fellowship of the USA and used by permission of InterVarsity Press, P.O. Box 1400, Downers Grove, IL 60515.

[4]*Ibid.*, p. 107.

[5]Taken from ORGANIZATION AND LEADERSHIP IN THE LOCAL CHURCH by Kenneth Kilinski and Jerry Wofford, p. 167. Copyright ©1973 by The Zondervan Corporation. Used by permission.

[6]*Ibid.*, p. 150.

[7]John Alexander, *Managing Our Work*. Downers Grove, IL: InterVarsity Press, 1975. p. 22.

[8]*Ibid.*, p. 54.

CHAPTER 10

Outreach
and Nurture

Evangelism must be defined in the local church context, not by the number of "prayers to receive Christ" or the number of "decision cards" signed. Unless an individual is incorporated into the life and ministry of the local church, it is questionable whether that individual has been evangelized in the New Testament sense. Dr. Win Arn pointed a finger at many of our traditional evangelical churches when he said,

> It is not enough to simply wish that decisions become established in the church . . . effective evangelism demands that the goal of making disciples and incorporating in the Body be a major platform of every mass evangelism crusade.[1]

Individuals who receive Jesus Christ must not be left alone in the wilderness of experience and cults. They must know the guidance and care of a local body of Christ that has been gifted to provide that kind of care. In that way alone can they become New Testament disciples. McGavran said, "Church growth people believe effective evangelism means making disciples and responsible members of Christ's church. Many methods of evangelism emphasize making *decisions*. Church growth people are concerned with making *disciples*." [2]

Blending and Bonding

Snyder has suggested that structure should provide a life-support system to encourage any newborn babe in Christ.

> All church structures should, in fact, help the church be the church and carry out its mission. They should be structures which promote community, build disciples and sustain witness. Structures which do this are valid: structures which do not are invalid, regardless of how esthetic, efficient or venerated they may be. [3]

Sources

The Chapel is committed to a multi-faceted approach to outreach, which is facilitated by the structures now in place. Once the individual is identified, he is linked up to a process that does not let him go until he is fully incorporated into his zone or shows no further interest.

1. *Visitors*. Individuals who visit our services are asked to fill out a visitor's card in the pew. They are also asked to stand and give their name and hometown. This is a fun time during the Chapel service, for often we will joke back and forth with the newcomer. We also have in the narthex a *Welcome Table*, where a visitor is encouraged to pick up a packet of information about the Chapel's ministries and a free book (usually a book on prophecy or the family).

2. *Men's breakfasts*. Once every two months we put on a breakfast for about 200 men, which features music, food, and a notable speaker. This speaker is usually a sports figure or an outstanding scientist. About 40% of those attending are not Chapel men. At the end of the breakfast an invitation is given; cards are in place for the

men to record their decision. Once they are identified, they are also linked up to the process.

3. *Women's ministries.* A group of women put on monthly meetings of an unusual nature—fashion shows, art exhibits, crafts, etc.—that attract outside women. Names from this group are also channeled into the process.

4. *Friendship evangelism.* Our Minister of Outreach has gone to our Body Life groups to instruct them in the philosophy of friendship evangelism. We see this as an important ministry. Seventy to eighty percent of our people came to the Chapel because a friend or relative invited them.

5. *Home Bible studies.* Approximately 25 home Bible studies are being taught and sponsored by Chapel people. This ministry also funnels new people into the Chapel.

6. *Discussion groups.* These are run mainly by the Senior Pastor. Whenever a zone feels that it can get together several non-Christian couples, we have an evening of questions and answers. This is not a Bible study, but a group that allows non-Christians to ask any questions they desire in a friendly and accepting atmosphere. These groups have proven extremely positive.

The Process

From whatever source the individual comes, once they have been identified they are plugged into the structure. We call this the *Blending and Bonding* process (see Figure 5). *Blending* refers to the incorporation of the new person into the Chapel (those who enter the "front door"), while *Bonding* refers to the cementing of relationships in fellowship and service (preventing exit through the "back door"). Let's take the simple example of a visitor who walks into the Chapel for the first time on a Sunday morning.

1. They are identified either by the card or by the Welcome Table.

2. A letter is sent out Monday morning by the Outreach Secretary.

3. The card is turned over to the particular zone in which the person resides and a "phoner" from that zone makes the first personal contact. The "phoner" asks the individual if they would like a visit. If so, then the outreach person from that zone makes the first visit. Information gained from the phone call and the visit is entered on the initial record sheet.

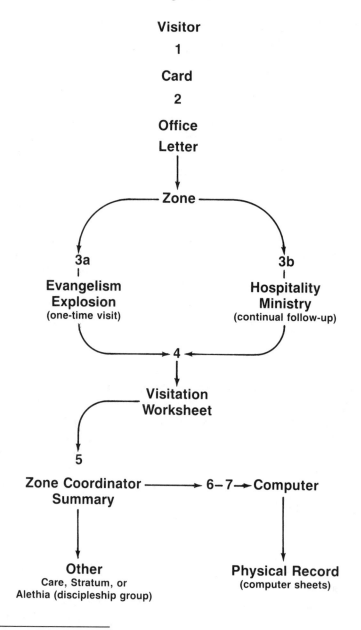

Figure 5. Jacksonville Chapel Visitor Response Process

If the new person does not want a visit, then the information gained by the phone call is still recorded, ready to be passed on. Should the phone call produce a totally negative response, then the name is dropped from consideration.

4. The information gained from the phone call or visit is returned to the Secretary of Outreach, who places the information on a visitation worksheet. She makes three copies of this information and distributes it to the staff, the board and, most importantly, to the Zone Coordinator.

5. The Zone Coordinator, after studying the information, determines how that individual should be served. Since he has at his disposal the ZIP panel, he may relay that person to Care, Outreach, or if young people are involved, to the Youth member of the ZIP Panel. These in turn establish further contact and try to encourage the newcomer in a particular ministry according to their needs.

6. Once that individual or family is actively attending and involved, the information is forwarded to the administrator of that zone.

7. That final piece of paper is returned to the pastor of zones, a staff member, who enters it into the computer. That final step sounds impersonal, but actually it has the opposite effect. In this manner, we can keep track of everyone in the Chapel and also have an instant mailing list and up-to-date information. For example, should College and Career need an updated list of all College and Career age people, we can provide one by printing out that age and interest. Should the board secretary need a list of all official members of the Chapel for a meeting, that is available at the push of a button. An updated Chapel directory is easy to produce because all of the names and addresses of the members are instantly available from the computer.

Nurture

One of the major complaints leveled at large churches is that they are impersonal, but such a problem is not indigenous to large churches. Most of us have had the experience of attending a small church that was cold and unresponsive.

Some of this criticism is valid, but coldness is not an inexorable consequence of bigness. The Zoning/Body Life and ZIP/ZAP structure serve to continue to provide a Biblical, nurturing ministry to the people. Apparently we are succeeding. A recent survey among our congregation indicated that the warmth and friendliness of the Chapel was exceeded only by the pulpit ministry as the reason why people remain at the Chapel once they come. That was listed ahead of other reasons such as choir, having personal friends here, and Bible school.

Once a person is placed into a zone, it becomes responsible for his care and nurture, along with the major ministries of the Chapel. Since the CAMEO structure is in place, the following is a description of the zone's ministry to newcomers:

CARE—The ministry of care may be a need for counseling, visitation, or even hospital concern. The Care ministry sees to it the service gets done.

ADMINISTRATION—This ministry organizes the affairs of the zone (special meetings, socials, etc.) and keeps track of the new individuals, handling any documents needed to help incorporate them in our ministry system.

MISSIONS—Each zone or Body Life group is assigned a particular missionary. The Chapel itself handles their financial support, but other needs like prayer, gift boxes, letters, and hospitality are handled in the zones. When the missionary is home, the Body Life group, through its Missions person, arranges for an appearance at a Body Life meeting and a place to stay. This activity keeps the subject of missions constantly before the zone.

EDUCATION—This ministry starts and becomes aware of Bible studies that are operating in the zones. Since this individual is a member of the major Education Committee, he is aware of the personnel needs in the major Chapel educational programs and helps fulfill those needs.

OUTREACH—This ministry is extremely important in the zoning program. Not only is it responsible to see that a new individual is visited, but also to develop outreach ministries within the zone itself.

In addition, the Youth ministry assists the Youth Pastor in the many activities offered by the Chapel and informs the individuals who have youth within their families of the major activities.

Each zone provides the personal touch that is necessary to maintain and nurture the families who come to us.

A major concern of the pastoral staff is to train these individuals. We provide counseling techniques for the Care people, management principles for the Administrative people, evangelistic training for the Outreach people, and so on.

Since each zone now contains at least three Body Life groups, there is a continual movement to create within these groups the five kinds of ministry people (CAMEO).

The threefold classification used by Mylander was *celebration, congregation, and cell.* We have used at times a more accurate description—Maxi-church (the major Chapel), Midi-church (the Zone), and finally the Mini-church (the Body Life groups). For a view of all three levels, see Appendix E.

Mylander devoted a chapter to losing people out of the "back door." They may attend and show interest, but if no interest is shown to them, they soon exit. Good sustained growth can happen only if the "back door" is closed. I believe we have provided a viable structure to achieve that. At the Mini-church level we have provided for counseling, prayer partners, and social events. The zones, at the Midi-church level, do the bulk of the work of keeping track of new people and involving them in ministry. We have also provided additional ministries in the central or Maxi-church.

The Sharing Room

Because New Jersey is a highly industrialized area, recession hits us severely. One of the Body Life groups became concerned about this and developed the idea of a "Sharing Room" in the Chapel, strategically located, stocked with food and dry goods. The room was obtained, freezers purchased, shelves installed, and the ministry was launched. It was headed up by one of the sensitive families in a Body Life group and was stocked voluntarily. Now families actually "shop" every Sunday after the morning service if they are facing financial crisis, and they can be counseled by social workers. The ministry continues to meet some very special needs.

The People Steeple

Seeing how much the Sharing Room helped, others began to envision the same kind of ministry with clothing. Another room was set aside to provide used but good clothing and household items. The room is kept well-stocked. Everything is cataloged by size, just like a department store. Families with small children are particularly attracted to this ministry. There is a major difference between the two: Anyone may use the People Steeple, while only those with a special need may use the Sharing Room.

Strata

Several years after our zoning ministries were in place and operating, we began to sense further needs. Zoning was a geographical grouping to expedite ministry within a certain geographical area, but we became increasingly aware of natural groupings that spanned all geographical zones. Junior High School, High School, and Young Adult groups had formed. Singles were becoming an important ministry. Taking a clue from what we had observed, we began to identify other need-groupings. A ministry was needed for seniors, one for young families with children, another for young couples.

We called these need groups "strata." The zone was a geographical grouping, and the strata was a need grouping. Obviously there would be overlapping. For example, a young family may be part of Zone 2 but they would have particular needs that might not be readily addressed in the overall zone. The same was true of singles and seniors. We also knew that each group needed their own CAMEO team to make a full-spectrum ministry available to them. Our finalized list was as follows: Junior High School, High School, Young Adults, Young Couples (without children), Young Families (with children), Singles (which included singles, widowed, divorced), and Seniors.

One wonderful couple in the Chapel, Bill and Merle Jeanne, had both been through very difficult divorces before they met and married. This, in a remarkable way, prepared them for their particular ministry. They are the Strata Coordinators for the Singles group and have created a powerful impact on the singles in North Jersey. At times the responsibilities are overwhelming, but let Bill tell about it:

Some time ago Merle Jeanne and I were asked if we would help start a Body Life group in Wayne; a Body Life group that would minister to the needs of some single people who were already meeting in a home there. That was four years ago and we are still meeting. If we had known then what our involvement would be we probably would not have accepted the challenge. But God, in His wisdom, knew what He had for us to do. The doors which that decision has opened for us are overwhelming. It is overwhelming to know that God has allowed us to have a part in the rebuilding of broken lives for His glory.

Recently the Singles have launched a special ministry to widows and widowers. The Young Couples have spawned a group for parents with adopted children. There was also a group for alcoholics and drug addicts.

All of this may sound overwhelming, but it is structure to facilitate ministry. When it is all boiled down, we have seven Zone Coordinators and seven Strata Coordinators, each with their own CAMEO teams. Out of all of this has come a real performance of ministry—and continuing challenges disguised as problems.

---

[1]Win Arn, *Church Growth Handbook.* Pasadena, CA: Institute for American Church Growth, 1979, p. 106.

[2]Donald McGavran, *Ten Steps for Church Growth.* New York: Harper & Row, 1977, p. 52.

[3]Taken from *The Community of the King* by Howard A. Snyder, p. 141. ©1977 by InterVarsity Christian Fellowship of the USA and used by permission of InterVarsity Press, P.O. Box 1400, Downers Grove, IL 60515.

CHAPTER 11

Fleshing
Out

"And the Word became flesh and dwelt among us." It seems that incarnation is one of God's favorite ways of communicating truth.

Jerry and Esther have been members of the Chapel with me since I first arrived as a new pastor in 1970. They live in Pompton Plains, New Jersey, approximately 45 minutes from New York City. They have five children, all of whom have now left home.

Jerry makes his living as a commercial artist (he works from a studio in his house), doing projects for major publications and publishers. He is a brilliant organizer and an in-depth, analytical thinker. Esther is an excellent partner in his life and ministry. She is a lovely, soft-spoken woman who extends the grace of God in her neighborhood by hosting breakfasts and luncheons and being involved in neighborhood Bible studies. Besides their zone ministry, they have taught kindergarten for 16 years.

Jerry and Esther are two people through whom the concepts in this book have been "incarnated" in the life and ministry of the Chapel, as this interview with Jerry shows.

Jerry, you've been involved in zoning from the start. How did these new concepts of distributing the ministry change your thinking?

The transition probably started in my heart before it ever made it to my head. I had been raised in some very strict and traditional churches and have served wherever I've lived. They each had a different kind of structure, a different type of organization, and different types of authority. Out of all those I recognized a void in my own life, which has nothing to do with my commitment to Christ, but more a question of how I could be effective in the local body. I gained new insights as to how God can work through an individual, making him a person who is worthwhile and has something to offer the rest of the believers and the world at large.

What do you know now that you didn't know then?

The big difference is that, when I look at an individual in whom Christ is working, I have a real sense of appreciation for that person—whether he is a baby Christian or has known and served Christ for a long time. The value of that person, gifted by the Holy Spirit, makes him someone very precious, someone to be reckoned with, someone to be developed, and especially a person with whom I can enjoy reciprocating in ministry.

You have been a Zone Coordinator for a long time. When you first began this process, did anything tangible confirm that this thinking was really Biblical?

As a Zone Coordinator I am in a special position where I can, over a long period of time, see God work in the hearts of people of all ages, and that has confirmed to me that God's promises are true.

I used to think that if someone had not come to Christ by the time they were finished with teenage years, or at the end of their teenage rebellion, they would be lost. What I have discovered is that people can discover and become babes even at age 35, 45, or 55, and there is an obvious, perceptible change in their lives, their relationship with their mates, their relationship with their children. The perceptible change is in what they think is important, what they decide to give, and what they decide to receive.

It is exciting to help people to develop, whether you call that discipleship or whatever, giving them the opportunity and encouraging them to exercise the gift that God has given them.

Let's look for a moment at your overall ministry. How many families are involved in your zone?

About 450 people from the Chapel live in my geographic area. I estimate that 60% of them attend the Chapel on Sunday morning *and* one other event during the week, whether choir practice, prayer meeting, Bible study, or Body Life. That's a high percentage, I think, for a "second-shot" involvement.

The demographics of families range from very young couples with no children to elderly people beyond retirement. There is no single layer of lifestyle. There are probably ten families represented in each of our six Body Life groups; these families are intensely involved in cell ministry and the business of sharing their spiritual gifts within the community. Another high percentage is the people who also serve the chapel centrally as Sunday school teachers, choir members, or volunteers of some sort.

Since you mentioned families, one of the focuses of at least three of our Body Life groups is to maintain family relationships—that is, not just a couples meeting on weekdays, but actually planning things and involving the whole family (aged parents and young children). The frequency of those events has really picked up over the last three years to the point where the children behave almost as though they are cousins. It is an exciting thing to see them actually look forward to getting together with their friends, their cousins.

Let's look at some individuals within your Body Life group who have been developed for ministry. Let's take a person like Johnny Cook. What was it that you saw in John and how did you see this eventually fulfilled?

John, as you know, is a sharer. Even before Christ made an impact on his life, I'm sure he would have given anybody anything they ever asked for. That trait remained a mark of John Cook. He was willing to have people borrow things and never return them. He would complain to me once in a while, but he would never complain to the individual. His home was also open. If you see mud inside a door, that usually means that person probably has an "open home and an open heart." I think it was so for John and Beulah. Their home was open.

If I had to look for people whom I would consider servants, that open door is my clue that they have a good view of people who live around them and people have a good view of them as well. They are the first to dip into their pocket after coffee, the first to open their home, the first to welcome people. They have few restraints on whom they are willing to associate with. I've thought a lot about that. If you are interested in a servant, it's the lady who does not mind the mud being tracked in on a winter night. When someone needs a place to meet, they open their homes; they deliver meals without a question when someone is sick; they enjoy having children around; they enjoy sharing all their possessions, all their privacy and even their priorities sometimes. They'll tuck aside a thing they think is important and put that on hold while they take care of a person.

I would say I have half a dozen people whom I could call right now and live at their house for a week, freeload off them, and they would not ask a question; or I could send someone to their home and they would take care of him. John typifies that kind of giving person.

What kind of people did he attract?

He attracted defective people; I think somehow he thought he had survived his own defects and I believe that he did. He had his hangups about his own worth, but I don't think he would ever say that. I personally took a risk with John when I gave him a slot and a "badge" to become involved as a Body Life leader. He would easily have made the "untouchable" list in almost every church I have been in before the Chapel. The man had a really rich life background. You could not fool him; he could see through any phony story in the world, but he let people do that to him and ministered to them anyhow.

He had a lot of very practical information and Biblical insight. The longer he survived in exploring his capabilities, the more wealthy he became in the things of the Lord and the more he got into the Word. The insights that he had were really remarkable and exciting.

He attracted people who had the same "checkered" history that he had and he treated them with dignity so they all benefited from their relationship with him. He had people in his Body Life group that no other group wanted or would tolerate, and everyone who came into that group benefited spiritually from him.

What about Sig Volz?

From the beginning he wanted to do it, and that made it easy for me, because all we did was discover ways that he would feel comfortable. Becoming involved as a kindergarten teacher was a lowly job, and he could not teach. He read only the German Bible. But what he could do was love, and his initial job was to take children in the kindergarten classroom who had no father in their home, and he played the father role for those children. He's been doing this ever since. The first class that he took are now juniors in college, and they still spot Sig when they come back and there are still little, trickling relationships with those juniors in college. He is still there and he is still doing it. Not only is he giving but he is faithful, dedicated, and loyal. He never forgets a friend and never forgets a relationship. He looks forward eagerly to the new set of four-year-olds who are going to be at his table in the fall.

That's the kind of heart Sig has. He has done the same thing with Body Life. He has generated more leaders than most other groups. He propels folks into the ministry.

He has become, unofficially, my assistant Zone Coordinator. Sig always focuses on the relationships between people and how, as children of God, these relationships should not be severed. He works very hard at networking people and getting people to respond to him and to God as well. He does not recruit; people respond to him as a whole person and he doesn't have to explain a lot to them. They are just willing to do what Sig asks them to do because they know he would not ask them anything that was improper or beneficial to the body. I give him free reign. I don't really tell Sig what to do; he invents it and we share and we "orchestrate." He is a free spirit and has really quality ideas.

Sig feels his home does not belong to him; it is not a private possession; he feels that God allows him to have the home. He built a special addition onto his home that comfortably seats thirty people. They have a pool. He and his wife are absolutely unselfish about any of that. Sig volunteers, ahead of me, to have an open house at Christmas, or after the Easter Cantata, or at Thanksgiving. The open house becomes a basis for continuing follow-up. People will show up there who will not come to the Chapel. They may have come from other churches or other denominations and so it is the largest possible "net" that we can arrange for fishing. People get caught in the net and love it. Because of his example, we have three other homes that have patterned their style.

What other ways do you reach out to your community?

When you think of CAMEO, outreach is the "O," but it can never stand alone. If we assume that outreach is eventually a clear presentation of the gospel, that has to be coupled with care and with education. They are almost inseparable. The fuzzy line between hospitality and outreach is difficult to perceive. Hospitality can sometimes be perceived as a waste of time and resources, unless it has an underlying intent to have someone's heart prepared to receive the gospel. That then becomes O plus C, outreach plus care.

A lot that I've heard has diminished the role of care, diminished the opening or softening of the heart, and jumped right into the outreach business. What seems to have worked in our case is a lot of care applied (care/hospitality attention). Go back to the flood. I believe hearts were softened towards what a church means in the time of tragedy and despair. That response is based on the care that we offered, the personalized attention given to people. That is appropriate and works well in time of tragedy and time of celebration; when a baby is born, or at the time of death. At those times people are vulnerable to the application of care as a ministry; if that is done, the next step is not so difficult when they are actually presented with the possibility of eternal life.

We have a least three Bible studies that are basically for non-Christian, people who have never heard anything or have heard something that was distorted. They are trying to reconcile what they heard with what we claim the Bible says. A lot of planning and personal effort goes into these Bible studies, which are considered an appendage of the zone ministry. Some of our ladies are expert at the business of education or reeducation to the point that people's hearts will be softened. Those ladies spend their time taking people who are either negative or ignorant of what Scripture has to say about their lives and walking gently, taking baby steps with those people. Some of them have gone on now for two or three years, and the net result is always amazing. Those ladies would probably not come to a breakfast or an open house; they are busy ladies who meet together once a week to prepare for the presentation of the gospel. They are waiting patiently for a response. That is another style of reaching people.

The nice part about the zone ministry is that we see those people at different times, in different places—at community events, school events, shopping. Those people are actually woven into our community life. Few secrets are left after you have either studied or fellowshiped together for a long period of time. They share a few family secrets, a few heartaches that are private and secret—once those all unravel, the person becomes vulnerable to the "infection."

Could you give a few specific examples of how your zone has reached out and ministered to families?

Need spans all levels of Christian maturity. You are a sitting duck for disaster, especially if you have children. My ministry starts out on the basis that I am a flawed person. I am an imperfect person and God loves me anyhow. I treat all people who are involved in cooperative ministry as flawed people, and I love them just the same. When that need strikes, it is not something that should be hidden from me. Surely God knows what it is already. If the need is shared with people who have that Christian's best interests at heart, then prayer is applied and good things happen.

People do not ever resign or leave because they ran into a "clinker" in their life or their child has humiliated them. The restoration process goes into effect immediately. People know how to pray and how to work through almost any imaginable problem, and they can and do once they realize that they have something to contribute to the hurting person.

Those needs can come into place when a child is stillborn; when an elderly parent is difficult to care for, and there is stress and torture when they have to be assigned to a nursing home; when there are too many small children in a home, and the mother has not enough energy or the capacity to deal with that; there is stress from parents dying. Our zone has faced all of those things.

When people have been tended to during those tragedies and survived, they have a wealth of experience and valid input that can then be shared with the next person. Survivors are precious; they are better than people who never were struck. We have survivors of long terminal illnesses, survivors of stillborn children, survivors where the father is unemployed and needs the help and support of others. The folks who belong to a praying group of people absolutely are ahead. They are survivors.

One example is the Johnson family. Phyllis took four years to die, and people stayed with her right up to the very end. She had a neighbor whose husband was in a similar dying process; they not only took care of Phyllis, but they moved next door and took care of that non-Chapel person.

Bob Vreeland works in a high-risk job. He is occasionally involved in high speed auto chases as a policeman. Some Body Life nights he's there and some nights he is not. Our prayer is always for him, and he has grown by leaps and bounds just because he was involved and realizes the power of prayer. All situations are bathed in prayer. A lot of personal energy and initiative goes into that.

What is it that makes your zone ministry so effective?

The term "coordinator" is really appropriate in my case because I don't let the job overwhelm me. If your ministry becomes a drudgery, either I've asked you to do the wrong thing or you volunteered to do the wrong thing. Anyone can take a break anytime they want to. They don't have to explain to me or anything. They can say, "You're not going to see me for a month," or six months or a year. You can't quit—God's work doesn't provide that alternative—but you are allowed to rest. There are no pledges, no signed statements, no promises. If you are willing and available, then we can work together. I think that kind of reciprocal relationship is what has made it go. It's what keeps people in place for a long period of time and longevity probably is the key.

I never lecture; I conduct private phone conversations or private breakfasts or private lunches. When we all do show up it's a sharing time, not a "let me tell you how it's going to be" session. When people get discouraged, I find it is because they have lost their perspective; they've forgotten where they were going or where they came from, and they don't know where they are. We talk about how God has worked through them in the past, how valuable they are, and how they really have something to contribute. They forget that so easily whenever times are tough. All I ask is that you recognize your gift and be willing to share it.

One of the other things I have been really careful about is that I don't take anything from it. I don't ask for anything, I don't expect anything, I don't take advantage of people. I've listened to the good stewardship testimonies of what people intend to sacrifice. I made a list of those things, and we sacrificed all of them about fifteen years ago. So it is in my mind a giveaway effort. God always gives it back. Because of my relationship with the people, I think I have earned the right to involve them in ministry, and they don't ever wonder about whether I have an ulterior motive.

What part in all this ministering process does the pastor play?

I have a way of getting from a pastor, my pastor, Earl Comfort, the same reaffirmation that I pass on to the people who work with me. You have never asked me for a promise or a pledge that I would be a good Zone Coordinator. What you've done is given me an opportunity, and you've never even called it a responsibility. You've given me a chance to exercise what God has given me and to pass it on, and I thank you for that.

I need to be reminded that there is a big picture out there somewhere and sometimes I forget that big picture. I especially appreciate the things that you, Earl, discover in Scripture. There is not a Sunday that goes by when you don't say something that touches upon the ministry that I'm trying to do. It's a living and vital business that we are involved in, absolutely not a structure, not an organization, not an event, not a program. It is here to stay and it is long-lasting. We are in a people process, and I'm glad to be a part of the process.

Jerry, what is it that really "rings your chimes" as a Zone Coordinator? What keeps you going?

I have a simple definition of success, and that is the capacity to share. If there is one key word that comes along with the responsibility of being a Coordinator, it is to *share*. That does not mean "giving," as most people would interpret, but also receiving, because you have to be able to share what other people have to offer. The reciprocal action of sharing indicates first of all that I have something to share. Whatever you claim as your spiritual gift can be shared. The thing that keeps me going is that other people do pick up on that. It's infectious. Sharing involves your heart, your ideals, your privacy. Sharing has a definite return. When it comes back in the form of other people sharing with you, then that to me is probably the most exciting thing.

Another interpretation of sharing is *trading*, but that doesn't work. If you do something in the form of ministry as a tradeoff, expecting to get something in return, trading and sharing are not the same. It is the "sharing business" that has been a benefit to myself, our family, our coupledness (with Esther). That's what "rings my chimes"—to see other people who are excited enough to share what God has given to them.

What encouraged Esther to be an active part of this whole ministry?

I think she probably encouraged *me* to be an active participant. First of all, she is a very giving person. She would give away everything we have if I didn't ask her not to. That's probably a key and a hallmark of all the people with whom we serve. I think probably the "couple" part is that I make suggestions sometimes where her ministry could best be expended, under the assumption that time is limited, our resources are limited, so I cooperate with her in sensing a direction or when I can see that the results will be what she hopes for—I can also pretty well sense when they won't be what she hopes for. So that's my gift to her; a sense of direction. As far as just being a good hostess, she is that. She networks people and does not take that lightly. It is not a need of hers to have people in the house, but she plans and prays for the right combinations of people. Amazing things happen when those people get together over a very simple breakfast or luncheon.

What is the bottom line, Jerry, the personal reward?

The reason I can say we are successful is that we enjoy sharing. We want to share, whether it is our time, our ideas, our money, our priorities, or our children.

God has definitely blessed us. I don't know where I'm going to work and what I'm going to do next year. I don't have a job, but somehow He always provides whatever we need, and we enjoy what we have and are not eager to accumulate more. That's how God has taken care of us. He has done it all these years, and I believe that He is going to keep on doing it. God has already given me more than I deserve, and I want to give out of His graciousness to me.

I look for that attitude in other people. Some people are serving God for other reasons, whether it is guilt or whatever. I want to work with people who are excited about ministry because God has already blessed them and they want to share that. Those are the people I like to recruit. I don't want you to come and work off your guilt in my program. The ones that really excite me are the ones who come saying God has given them far more than they ever deserved and they are stymied because they either can't get started or they can't understand what the value of that is. To me that is an exciting person to work with, and I would drop everything and work with that person. Esther would too. That really is what our ministry is—helping people do their ministry and never letting it fall through the cracks.

CHAPTER 12

Getting Started

Jean accepted Christ at one of our discussion groups and began growing immediately. Soon after, she went through a difficult pregnancy and when her baby boy was born, a heart problem surfaced with him that required open heart surgery. During this time Jean was also notified that her mother had been killed in a car accident. Yet through all this Jean maintained her testimony and continued to grow. Christians from her group ministered to her and supported her in prayer and in some very practical ways. This ministry made a special impact on one special person in her life — her husband. Jean's words are best:

> During this time my husband sat back and took in all of what was happening around us. He saw Chapel friends come to us and visit, calling to see how we were and if we needed anything. He heard them

talk about praying, he ate the meals they had cooked for us and accepted their gifts, and answered the phone calls from the ministers. Well, three months after my son's surgery, my husband asked me to call one of the pastors to come by for a talk. He came and Joseph accepted Christ.

The testimonies and stories are legion. New "war stories" come in every day. Our minister of Pastoral Care is a storehouse brimming with excitement and can be tapped at any time to share what is happening "in the trenches." It is truly amazing to behold.

Facing Change

When I came to the Jacksonville Chapel in 1970, it had a board of forward-looking men. I had come from a pastorate in which there was very little organizational vision or challenge. However, new ideas of ministry and discipleship were stirring in my head. I would be working with new men, some of whom were top-level executives who would share with me their experience in tackling organizational problems. At the time the church had less than 300 people. It now has between 1200 and 1300 people, but I believe there is more close-knit fellowship and more interpersonal ministry now than there was when we were smaller.

Preparation for Change

Since it takes time for even a pastor to readjust his ideas, then obviously time should be given to a congregation and to its leadership. Much damage has been done by young visionaries who, in bringing much-needed change, rush in "where angels fear to tread." Christians often ascribe to the traditional organizations a sanctity of being Spirit-inspired, and they would just as soon surrender Wednesday night prayer meetings as their Scofield Bibles. They may not *use* either, but both are treasured just the same. Getz, an innovator himself, warns of the resistance to change.

> That does not mean that there will not be those who will resist change. It is natural among all people whether Christian or non-Christian. Management studies show that about 10% of a group of people in an organization are *innovators*—people willing to try almost any new form or

structure or idea. About 80% are *conservative* — people who are hesitant to change, until they have all the facts and have their feet firmly planted on projections that seem to be completely feasible. Only about 10% are *inhibitors* — people who are against any kind of change, whether they have the facts or not.[1]

Since I anticipated this kind of resistance, I spent approximately a year and a half studying the book of Ephesians with the congregation, laying the Scriptural foundation not only in my own mind but in the minds of my people. I also circulated significant books among my leaders. Personal conversations helped open many closed minds. We were now ready for some changes.

When other churches discover what we have been doing at Jacksonville Chapel, they often want to place an organizational structure similar to it upon their own local church situation without proper Biblical preparation. Saul's armor fit Saul but not David. To impose an innovative structure borne out of years of progressive understanding upon a traditionally structured church is to invite irritation, abrasion, and eventual failure. I've seen this happen to churches that were not adequately prepared by proper Biblical perspectives. We did not begin to make changes until a one-and-one-half-year study had been given to the church at large on certain Biblical texts that provided the underpinning so necessary for change.

An Approach for Smaller Churches

The distribution of ministry, whether using CAMEO or another method, is entirely applicable and workable in smaller congregations. This is not a general approach geared only to larger churches with staff and personnel adequate to support it.

First and foremost, as with larger congregations, the Biblical foundation of a gifted ministry must be laid. Before any congregation attempts to arrange *what* to do, it must address the question of *why* to do it. Texts such as Ephesians 4 and Romans 12 should be studied and understood by the leadership. Unless pastor and leadership are committed to these concepts, all restructuring efforts will be in vain. A series of messages to the entire congregation on the Bible texts on the body gifted for ministry is the only foundation upon which a successful restructuring can be made.

The next logical step is the creation of some kind of home groups in which face-to-face sharing in ministry would take place. This would accomplish two important things: 1) It would help people to realize that there are great needs among them; 2) it would encourage them when God actually uses them in some way to meet those needs. However, those groups should be aware that they will not be immediately successful (ours were not) and that they will be heirs of many discouragements and problems. The early problems we experienced are listed elsewhere in this book. However, out of these initial groups many will experience not only the giving but also the receiving of ministry.

The next major step should be taken at the board level. The pastor could conceivably serve as coordinator of his own congregation and enlist his board to serve as a CAMEO team. That would initially involve himself and five board members. Each of these board members could enlist their close friends to help them with their respective ministries.

Let me illustrate. Suppose the pastor-coordinator is notified of someone in the hospital. This happens almost daily in any pastorate. He would contact the Care board person and make him aware of the need. As an initial step, that board member could accompany the pastor to the hospital. Then after the visit, they might discuss what the immediate needs are: financial, meals for the family, or transportation of some kind. They in turn could recruit other members of the Care team to help alleviate these needs. Imagination and creativity can take over from here.

Perhaps a missionary is about to speak to the congregation. The pastor-coordinator would contact his Missions team member about the occasion and suggest that he arrange a simple "Potluck Missions Dinner." The missionary might also need overnight accommodations. With every need, more and more people are being acquainted with the opportunity for ministry. Applications, even at this smaller level, could indeed be exciting.

All of this serves to make the Biblical concepts of ministry alive and exciting. When growth begins to take place (and I'm certain it will), the prejudice toward an every-member ministry would already be in place. In fact, I seriously believe it would be easier to implement these concepts with a smaller congregation than a larger one, because a larger one requires an organizational overload that would be troublesome. There would also be an advantage of strong pastoral input at this smaller level. Pastors and leaders would grow together.

Looking Ahead

Someone remarked recently, "The future ain't what it used to be." Perhaps that's a reflection of the potential disasters that exist around us. But the church should never subscribe to such a statement. Certainly we don't feel that way. With the experience we have already gained with our structure, we are very excited about future possibilities.

Short-Term Goals (2-3 years)

1. We intend to strengthen the zone concept through staff training and utilization. We also plan to have pan-zone meeting so that the coordinators can share what they have done and provide cross-pollination.

2. We seek to provide a greater autonomy in the zones. As early attempts succeed, we can provide evaluation and guidance so that the zone leaders and the panels will become more and more confident.

3. We seek to stimulate greater evangelization at a local level. We are concluding several pilot programs that will give us data for future evangelistic attempts:

—One zone has invited a top research scientist who is a Christian for a special lecture series in their municipal building. They have sent out special mailings to everyone in town (4800), inviting them to the meeting. The Chapel provides the finances, the design and counsel, but the zone will stage the entire event. The Chapel is also helping with the follow-up.

—Another zone was targeted for a special doorknob hanging campaign. An attractive Thanksgiving brochure was designed, offering an invitation to the community to join us for a special Thanksgiving service.

—Another zone is planning a "Welcome Wagon" approach for their residents.

These attempts at outreach at the local level will be evaluated and the resultant information will be used to share with other zones.

4. Procure new staff members who understand and feel comfortable with the philosophy of training zone people.

5. Even though our entire Chapel is now on computer, we plan to update so that each individual has fresh information logged with his identity. All we would have to do is print out a name and a profile would appear. This procedure would enable us to "track" an individual more closely.

Long-Term Goals (5 years)

1. Numerically, we can look forward to ten zones with about 200 family units within each zone, which would likely total about 5000 people. If we do our jobs well, we should have about ten Body Life groups per zone, each functioning effectively as a mini-church.

2. Our internship program should be in full swing. This plan envisions bringing recent seminary graduates on board and having them train with us for three years. By that time, we can spin them off into local churches who need pastors. We would offer to pay part of their salaries for the first year or two. We could also start new congregations in outlying areas (beyond ten miles). These interns would have the Chapel philosophy along with sound Biblical doctrine.

3. We must strive for a constant, close liaison between Board Chairman, Committee Chairman, Pastoral Staff, and Zone Coordinators for intense goal-setting and planning subsequent to the general work being completed by the staff and the Steering Committee. We must make sure that our movement to the future is a "symphony" production and not a simple "tuning up" time in which one does not know what the other is doing.

Conclusion

A final word of caution is necessary. What I have presented in the previous chapters is simply how one church, over a period of years, put together a structure to express a Biblical philosophy of ministry—mainly the distribution of ministry to God-gifted people.

This, above all, is not a gimmick to be superimposed on churches without special Biblical preparation and a sensitivity to prevailing cultures and ecclesiastical limitations. Supremely, it should never be considered as a substitute for what I believe to be the heartbeat of any local church situation—an effective pulpit. It is the pulpit that originally prepared the people for such a ministry and it is the pulpit that sustains them for this continued kind of approach.

When both an effective pulpit and an emphasis upon the distribution of the ministry are joined in an exciting marriage, the children of such a union are growth and godliness. Organization is not a substitute for a strong pulpit, but then too a strong pulpit cannot exist alone, for then the church becomes an audience. When the latter problem develops—the exclusion of personal ministry—then Christians become unresponsive, critical, and increasingly sterile. The most responsive group of people in all the body are warriors who, wounded and bruised in battle, find the spiritual medication to heal them and place them once again into the fray.

May their tribe increase!

---

[1]Gene Getz, *Sharpening the Focus of the Church*. Chicago, IL: Moody Press, 1975, p. 256.

Appendix

A. Sermon Outline and Worksheet

Jacksonville Chapel
Dr. Earl V. Comfort   1 Peter 3:13-18
"THE HELP OF HOPE"

I.   INTRODUCTION

    A.   John, Charles, Sylvester and Chuck

    B.   Injustice
        1.   a common problem
        2.   an opportunity

            the church is to _____
            the church is to _____

IF GOD IS	THEN I AM
Loving	
Just	
Sovereign	

  C.   Resource in Frustration
     THEME: *In the midst of the frustrating circumstances of life the Christian is* _____
     by the unshakable _____ *that they are temporary, meaningful and overcome by the power of God.*

II.   BODY

    A.   **SUFFERINGS ARE TEMPORARY**

        1.   The Work of Christ
            a.   a universal problem
            b.   an amazing contrast
        2.   The Whole Problem
        3.   The Christian's "Once"

    B.   **SUFFERINGS ARE MEANINGFUL**

        1.   A Common Complaint
        2.   An Alarming Inference
        3.   A Glorious Conclusion

    C.   **SUFFERINGS ARE OVERCOME BY THE POWER OF GOD**

        1.   A Puzzling Phrase
        2.   A Comforting Confidence

III.   CONCLUSION

SUFFERINGS

B. Ministry Designations

Care

Benevolence
Blood Drive
Body Life
Counselors
Coupon Exchange
Hospitality
Marriage Plus
People Steeple
Sharing Room

Administration

Chapel Picnic
Coffee Table
Equipment
Facilities
Finances/Purchasing
Kitchen
Land
Nursery School
   (Finances)
Staff/Office
   Management

Missions

Application of Funds
Missions Conference
Scholarships

Education

Adult Bible School
Bible School
Books/Literature
Instructional
   References
Library
Nursery School
   (Education)
Vacation Bible School

Outreach

Advertising
Discussion Groups
Home Bible Studies
Media
Men's Breakfasts
Special Events
Visitation
Welcome Table

Youth

Brigade
Kids for Christ
Pioneer Girls

Worship Support

Chapel Players
Flowers
Gospel Gang
Music
Nursery
Sound
Tape Ministry
Ushers

Staff

"Chapel Light"
Films
New Members
Speakers

Strata

College and Career
Singles
Seniors
Women's Ministries
Young Adults
Young Couples
Young Families
Youth

C. Zone (Stratum) Coordinator Ministry Description

I. PHILOSOPHY

A. Assumptions

1. All ministry functions are best attended by those whose service is the exercise of a spiritual gift, not an obligation to a duty roster.

2. The clustering of gifts into our "CAMEO" spectrum is a reasonable and biblically consistent approach.

3. A logical understanding of people within the cultural framework of the Chapel constituency is on the basis of where they live (community) and the stage of life they have reached (lifestyle). We have chosen two terms, "zones" and "strata" to designate these ways of considering people.

4. A stratum and a zone are complementary, not competitive. Each has unique characteristics to consider when ministering to people.

5. The Chapel's primary purpose is to distribute a full-spectrum ministry (CAMEO) to its people in *coordinated* fashion (Ephesians 4:1-16), so that it will "contend as one man for the faith of the gospel" (Philippians 1:27), with each one becoming perfect in Christ (Colossians 1:28)

B. Coordinator Qualities

1. Qualifies as an elder in his personal life.

2. Agrees with Chapel doctrine and bylaws (same as membership qualifications).

3. Cooperates with Chapel leadership in the processes toward outreach, growth, maturity, ministry, and the distribution of the ministry (CAMEO) to his assigned people at the "cell" level, the "midi-congregation" (zone/stratum) level, or at the large "celebration" level.

4. Has a heart for people and a particular empathy for the people of his zone or stratum.

5. Senses God has equipped him with qualities to be used to serve his zone or stratum.

II. DUTIES
A. Assists in the selection of his CAMEO panel to aid in the distribution of the ministry.
B. Sees to the well-being of his CAMEO people.
C. Calls his panel and other organizational heads in his zone (stratum) together for prayer, fellowship and coordinated activities for the well-being of his zone.
D. Coordinates the distribution of CAMEO ministries to his zone through his panel.

III. ACCOUNTABILITY
A. Looks for help and direction through the pastoral contact person from the board.
B. Seeks to cooperate with other Chapel zone and stratum coordinators for the welfare of the Chapel.

D. Definitions and Terms

1. **Pan-Chapel Groupings:**
   Maxi-Congregation: 2000+ Attenders ("Celebration")
   Midi-Congregation: 200+ Attenders (Zone/Stratum)
   Mini-Congregation: 20   Attenders (Body Life Group)

2. **Stratum:** A life-phase classified by its unique concerns, needs, and resources, but not necessarily by age. These phases, through which maturing people pass, are identified by generic terms (young marrieds, singles, seniors, etc.) A stratum is a midi-congregation (potentially 200+ attenders).

   Zone: A geographically defined midi-congregation.

3. **Coordinator:** A layman who brings a balanced emphasis of the full-spectrum ministries to a midi-congregation (Zone or Stratum) through the cooperative efforts of his CAMEO panel.

4. **Panel Person:** A layman or couple managing one facet of the spectrum by directing and discipling like-gifted cell leaders. A conduit for pan-chapel resources and communications, "up and down."

5. **Committee:** A division of the trustee board, responsible for the effectiveness and availability of a singular ministry's policies, procedures, resources, plans, and goals.

6. **Pastor:** A full-time staff person called to be an *equipper,* to recruit, train, and encourage all levels of lay ministry within a singular CAMEO facet, and a *shepherd* to an assigned midi-congregation (especially its lay leadership) as a spiritual advisor.

7. **CAMEO Ministry Facets:** Clusters of spiritual gifts exercised by individuals and teams to reflect the attributes of God toward the maturing of disciples and increasing attendance.

   Care—Hospitality/Compassion for needy/Fellowship bonding
   Administration—Organization/Personnel/Facilities/Finance
   Missions—Concern for the lost beyond our reach
   Education-Discipling through Biblical precepts and their
      application
   Outreach—Concern for the lost within our reach

8. **Programs:** Classes, studies, or meetings (Sunday school, for example) conducted regardless of group size or CAMEO ministries exercised. Programs are not Strata or Zones! Strata and Zones are *people,* not programs.

E. Three Levels of Structure—an Overview

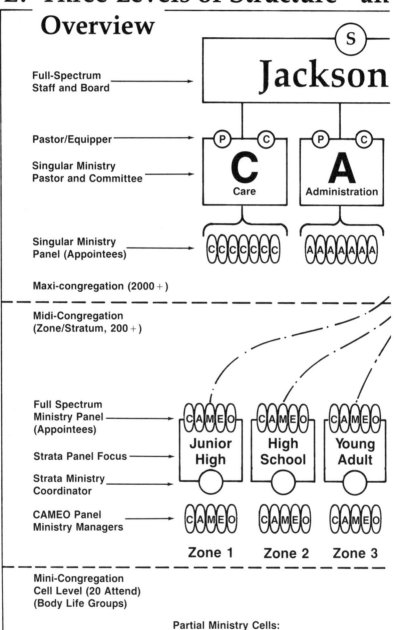

Full-Spectrum Staff and Board

Pastor/Equipper

Singular Ministry Pastor and Committee

Singular Ministry Panel (Appointees)

Maxi-congregation (2000+)

Midi-Congregation (Zone/Stratum, 200+)

Full Spectrum Ministry Panel (Appointees)

Strata Panel Focus

Strata Ministry Coordinator

CAMEO Panel Ministry Managers

Mini-Congregation Cell Level (20 Attend) (Body Life Groups)

Partial Ministry Cells:
Classes, studies, groups, programs,

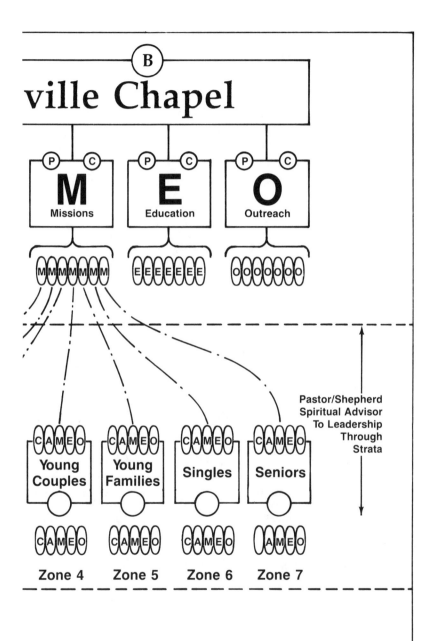

events, activities, seminars, banquets, etc.

F. An Overview of the Outreach Ministry

I. Philosophy

    A. Outreach is a *critical* element of Christian maturity.

    B. Outreach mandate is primarily to

        1. Create an atmosphere for ministry.

        2. Equip for ministry.

    C. Outreach ministries should be designed to involve more, not fewer, people.

II. Assumptions

    A. Christians can do outreach as they are. Sometimes "natural" outreach is even best.

    B. *Outreach* is "influencing people to become Christians."

III. Structure

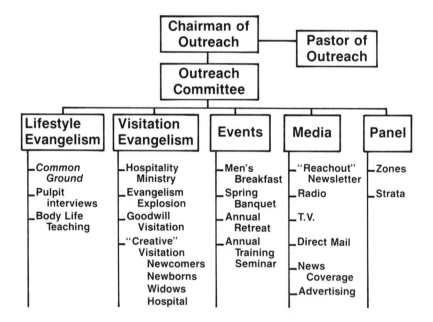

Index